Demons
On Her Shoulder

K T BOWES

Copyright © 2014 K T BOWES

All rights reserved.

ISBN-10: 1500931144
ISBN-13: 978-1500931148

DISCLAIMER

This is a work of fiction. Names, characters, businesses, places, events and incidents are either the products of the author's imagination or used in a fictitious manner. Any resemblance to actual persons, living or dead, or actual events is purely coincidental.

All rights reserved. No part of this book may be reproduced in whole or in part without the express written permission of the author.

This work is the intellectual property of the author writing as K T Bowes..

OTHER NOVELS BY K T BOWES

The Hana Du Rose Mysteries based in NZ:
About Hana
Hana Du Rose
Du Rose Legacy
The New Du Rose Matriarch
One Heartbeat
The Du Rose Prophecy

NZ Teen Mayhem Series:
Free From the Tracks
This Too Shall Pass
Blaming the Child

Novels based in England:
Artifact

ACKNOWLEDGMENTS

I wish to acknowledge those who work hard to protect the sanity of victims of sexual abuse, especially at those times when they are in no position to guard it for themselves.
That covers anyone who willingly gets involved, from professional organisations to shocked family members and friends. Nobody is immune from the far reaching fingers of destruction, but all can survive them if we just stick together. To the beautiful city of Lincoln, I grew up in the folds of your stone arms and ran when my childhood was lost. Yet when I returned you welcomed me, like we were old friends.

Cover Image
The photograph of the central tower of Lincoln Cathedral is courtesy of © Copyright Allan Chapman and licensed for reuse under Creative Commons Licence.

PROLOGUE

The figure glowered down from his throne in the rafters as the minions circled submissively in the darkness. His stone grimace remained fixed on the tiny face, but he worked the room with his personality, dividing and conquering admirably while stirring up trouble and misery. *Anger* fluttered down nervously, daring to fly closer than *Grief* or *Guilt*, seeking approval but fearing reprisals. The stone figure was rigid and still, hundreds of years of pent up aggression stored in the grey statuesque body. Yet the demons remembered it well, the mocking, sarcastic laugh and the terrifying violence. They jostled and jockeyed in front of the imp, not caring that they gored each other with knotted, clawed hands and *Despair* took a clumsy swipe at *Bereavement's* gnarled ears, cackling with mirth as distracted he flew into a stone pillar. *Depression* hissed at them in warning, his cloying misery leaving a bitter aftertaste that hung in the air. The sons of *Death* circled in a moth-like dance of worship and adoration, feeling the vibrations in the atmosphere that signified that the others were coming. They would come to pay the Lincoln Imp homage in his enforced stasis, understanding that it could not last forever. The glorious and terrible day would come when he would be free to rove the earth once more and pick his own victims. Until then, his children would do it for him.

The drone of approaching wings grew louder. As *Murder* and *Violence* folded leathery wings on the lead roof of the cathedral, the lesser demons received their orders and fled. The sightless, unblinking eyes of the figure perched high on the stone pillar were intense and glaring as yet more sons paid him a visit.

The demons stayed together as they flew south, invisible to the sleeping city below. But their familiar aura covered the area as unsuspecting residents awoke to feelings of inexplicable heaviness and foreboding. The creatures fought and argued for dominance as they landed on a balcony in the oldest part of the city, sensed by a nocturnal ginger cat who hissed and spat at their combined foulness. Eager to begin their meddling and wanting to be first to assail their chosen victim, the demons stalked excitedly into the upstairs apartment and began the daily, psychological torture on which they thrived.

CHAPTER ONE

The clamour of irrepressible sobbing erupted suddenly and without warning. Jayden kept her demure face neutral as the overweight client in front of her crumpled into the swollen armchair like a deflated airbed. The tissues were a fraction to the left of her seat, easily within reach. A jug of cold water condensated quietly on the coffee table next to three robust looking glasses.

Jayden kept very still, not wanting to halt the spell. It had taken weeks to get to this point and she had begun to doubt herself. Long, intensely frustrating hours of pushing the knotty issue around and around in a giant, self-defeating circle, which had the potential to go exactly nowhere. The demons sat figuratively on the large woman's shoulder, unseen but unquestionably there and undeniably felt. *Grief. Bitterness. Rejection.* Sinking in their claws and patting at her shoulder with their filthy, clammy hands. Jayden knew them well. She had those of her own whom she managed periodically to wrestle off and bind, but they invariably returned when she wasn't looking, or when remembered pain made her forget to close the doors of her heart.

The box of tissues began to slide towards the leaking woman, slowly at first but picking up momentum as sobbing wracked her body and set it almost out of control. Her whole frame shook and wobbled in the chair like an oversize pink blancmange being carried too roughly and Jayden feared that her client might pitch out of its depths and onto the floor. The tissues reached the end of the table and became visible to the woman as she swiped the back of her hand across her sticky nose. Jayden watched her carefully. Desperation oozed out of every pore as her brokenness became raw and open in all its cancerous horror. The transformation was painful and tragic to watch, but it was well overdue. With shaking manicured hands, the poor wife reached out and snatched the uppermost tissue and realising quickly that it wasn't enough, made a swift grab for another five.

Liquid poured distastefully from every facial orifice, a year's worth of poisonous anguish leaking out finally from the blonde woman's pain-encrusted soul and it would not be ceasing any time soon. From the matching chair next to her, a hairy hand reached out for the water jug and poured a halting stream of icy refreshment into the clean glass nearest. A tremor in the stubby fingers made the water slosh slightly as he helpfully held it up to his companion's face.

The crying ceased instantly. The woman turned her face slowly to the left, snot and tears running like a coloured waterfall down her face, uniting with mascara and foundation wherever it touched. Her movements were slow and the man should have seen it coming. But then he should have seen a lot of things coming and hadn't. She grasped the glass in her sodden fingers and Jayden's eyes widened as she read the unveiled emotion in her client's puffy face. The water cascaded into the man's eyes, arcing gracefully through the air. The glass followed it, thudding hard into his forehead but surprisingly didn't smash. As it fell to the floor with a muted thump on the thick pile maroon carpet, the woman leapt nimbly to her feet and began pounding his head, neck, chest and face, dodging his outstretched arms skilfully like a flyweight boxer.

Jayden exhaled and wondered when to break it up. It was not uncommon in a case such as this. There were no other likely weapons within easy reach, but it didn't matter anyway as the woman had begun crying again slumped over the man who was now pinned to the chair. He was stretching his arms around her wide frame and patting her back gently as though she was a child. Without making a sound, the counsellor got up from her comfy chair and exited the room, leaving the door slightly ajar. She walked confidently to the kitchenette behind the reception desk and began to make hot drinks; a pot of tea for the women and coffee for him.

Jayden bashed the tea bags around the inside of the pot with a teaspoon, avoiding the scalding hot water and loading the tray with drink paraphernalia. She wondered why she had been so reluctant to ask that appropriately significant question and wished that she had done it weeks ago. *"How did your husband's affair make you feel?"*

CHAPTER TWO

"Night, Sal," Jayden called cheerfully to the receptionist as she closed her office door, locked it and walked towards the ill-fitting glass exit. Sal waved back enthusiastically, blonde hair bobbing on a pale face and nodded towards Campion's closed door. Evidently their colleague was still in his four o'clock session. He wasn't great at time keeping, but Jayden hoped that he wasn't having problems. At six feet four inches tall and a black belt, he wasn't likely to be out of his depth, not physically anyway. He could always buzz for Sal if things got out of hand. He hadn't yet, not in eight years of working there. Japanese genetics carefully blended with the frame of a football line-backer made him an interesting combination of distinctive features.

"Jayden! I'm glad I caught you!"

"You didn't," came Jayden's brusque retort, administered without turning around. "I've finished for the day."

"Yes but, I..." the vicar commenced again, running to reach her before she got safely to the exit and took flight like a slender blackbird, "about before, it was..."

Jayden turned her lithe body in his direction, giving him her full attention. Lengthy dark hair cascaded down her back in boisterous waves and her startling green eyes bore into him as she moved to regard his earnest, florid face. The force of her presence knocked the man off his determined stride slightly and gave her the break she needed. She leaned in towards his elegantly robed body in a threatening manner. "If you disrupt our appointment schedule in that way again, I will walk out that door and never come back!"

The vicar gulped and his penguin-like attire fluttered around behind his portly frame as he shifted nervously in the wake of Jayden's hostility. "Cam and I have told you repeatedly that you are more than capable of dealing with initial counselling on your own. All you have to do is take basic details and refer them to us. What you did today was unprofessional! Marching that poor girl and her parents in here like that! Cam is now still trying to catch up on the people who were left waiting. He and I also had a couple's counselling session booked and I was forced to do it by myself, because it was too late to put them off. The woman turned violent and I was on my own. Because of you!"

Jayden punctuated her sentence with a well-timed finger jab and watched the astonishment in the vicar's flaccid face turn to guilt while she milked it for all it was worth. She only hoped that he would take notice this time and stop his dangerous practices. "I will have to tell my supervisor about this and the bishop may well need to get involved. I can't work in these conditions and nor can poor Cam!"

"But the girl was p..." the vicar leaned conspiratorially forwards, his chins wobbling fit to fall off and Jayden put her hand decisively into his face to silence him. The receptionist was discreet, but all clients had an undisputed right to confidentiality.

"I'm not discussing it now. I'm going home." Jayden strutted through the glass doors and out into the winter evening, aware that the vicar was staring after her crossly.

The Reverend John McLean contemplated Jayden's retreating figure for a moment as his white hair fluffed up in the breeze from the slamming metal framed doors. He considered the possible ramifications of what she had threatened. A complaint to the bishop would go badly for him, especially as the new incumbent had not yet taken up his post formally. Reverend McLean was desperate for an excuse to meet his new superior and size him up, but *this* incident would not be an advisable pretext. The new bishop had not yet settled in the city, unexpectedly held up in the north of the country but he was meant to be in post very soon.

McLean's bulbous, red-veined nose wrinkled with the thought of greeting him for the first time and he wondered whether the congratulatory card addressed to the diocesan office in Harrogate had reached him yet. Bishop Pargetter's hasty resignation following a major heart attack had been unplanned and left a flying bishop in charge. McLean personally felt that the stand-in was incompetent, but no matter. Not much longer to wait. He and Pargetter had been old chums from seminary and had fortuitously allowed McLean's archaic modus operandi to function without criticism. He placed a ragged nail between thin, unsmiling lips and wondered how he would fare with a new superior. No more whiskey chasers in the expensively furnished lounge with an old friend. Surely there was nothing to worry about. St Jude's was refreshingly free of the usual riff-raff which clung around the edges of Christian communities. He made sure of that. It was a nice safe church with nice safe people and the new man would see that instantly and be thrilled with the current no-nonsense values.

In the Reverend's mind, *his* problem was simply that the world had changed too quickly for the old vicar and his role had cascaded down the moral chute with it. It felt as though one minute he was chatting to fresh-faced newlyweds and baptising fluffy, pink babies and the next it was all homosexuality, terminal illness, tragedy and pregnant teenagers. It had happened overnight, like a slap to the face and caught him seriously napping.

The Reverend McLean was a hard taskmaster, not because he was rough or dictatorial but because he was pretty much inept at just about everything. He had an image of himself which was wildly inaccurate and created chaos without bounds. Then with a wailing and gnashing of teeth, he would expect everyone around him to clear up his mess and put the world straight again, emerging with a smile and expecting congratulations. He was not a natural manager by any stretch of the imagination and how the previous bishop had seen fit to give him St Jude's to destroy, two decades previously, nobody who knew him could fathom. He seemed to have landed on his feet purely by default and that ever-present phenomenon in which dross invariably rises to the top. If demons could be attributed to him, then *Pride, Avarice* and *Deceitfulness* would be found riding high on his shoulders, jostled regularly out of the way by *Prejudice*.

The Reverend John McLean sincerely believed that everyone loved him. He smiled and simpered and threw the occasional, highly inappropriate sweets at his employees in an attempt to buy them off. For one, it would be a decorated office when they had requested a new computer, for another, an afternoon off when they had requested help. For those in real difficulty, it might be an insincere kindly spoken word just before they burst a blood vessel and left, retired or expired. His monotone monologues, coupled with his tendency to treat everyone as though they were an expectant five-year old, had succeeded in successfully decimating a previously thriving church and ruining a fairly solvent business.

Fortunately, the counselling offices were run and paid for by the diocesan administration, so he couldn't directly destroy their success notwithstanding the fact that he had tried. McLean loved to run with a megalomaniacal management style, in which nobody else knew what was going on except him and half the time he wasn't completely sure either. He wrangled for long hours over minutiae, searching for the right sort of red rug for his office for weeks. He returned from the shops with a blue one that successfully legged everyone up and ended up in the toilets. Meanwhile, the church organist's cancer snatched her from under his nose without a single hospital visit from him. And then, his primary consideration was who he could coerce to replace the poor woman and the inconvenience to him personally. To listen to him now, you would think that she had died deliberately just to make work for him as a last act of spite.

McLean played 'favourites' diligently and with real skill, elevating and disposing of employees and congregation members without a backward glance. One week they were 'marvellous, amazing, irreplaceable' while the next, they were 'useless, irritating or so-last-year' without any discernible warning, discarded easily in exchange for a new toy which could perform to order. Curates came and curates left, arriving fresh faced and excited about their calling and leaving depressed, suicidal and neither use nor ornament for anything else. Curates who passed through the Reverend McLean's ample fingers didn't just flee from his church, they abandoned their faith on the doormat as they wiped their sensible shoes on the way out. Loyalty came at the cost of the one freely offering it. But its loss; the shuddering terminal withdrawal of it from one who had failed to recognise its benefit w too terrible to contemplate. The Reverend McLean's ineptitude simply turned such tearing pain into *their* betrayal of *him*, engendering hatred for the person whose abandonment, he felt keenly somewhere deep within his psyche.

John McLean sighed heavily and thought of his wife. She was desperate for him to retire to their little house on Skegness seafront. Perhaps he should give it consideration instead of smiling sagely and placating her with weekend visits. Unless he could extricate himself from this latest drama, it might be an enforced leave of absence. He pulled a nasty face, rather as though he had been sucking on a lemon and pondered his options. He was a shrewd man concerning his own progression and advancement. Shrouded effectively under the veil of incompetence, it usually guaranteed him getting what he wanted. Unfortunately not with the counsellors. With them he seemed confusingly out of his depth, especially the haughty female who clearly needed a good mate to calm her down. The reverend swished around with a squeak of his sensible brown Hush Puppy shoes on the stone floor and went in search of his curate.

"Briiiiaaaannn!" he called eerily into the empty church, enjoying Brian's discomfort around him recently. "Stupid little man," the reverend whispered into the growing darkness, hearing his words echoing back to him. "Briiiaann."

Brian, the rotund, balding male was likely to be found in the vestry, his chunky legs resting nonchalantly on the desk with tomato sauce stains on his black shirt. Only yesterday, Reverend McLean had caught him swigging communion wine and listening to the dog racing on a portable radio. He realised that some degree of blame could rest on his own sloping shoulders; after all, he was meant to have mentored the young cleric at some point in the previous ten years. But life inevitably got in the way and the curate sought attention like a naughty teenager, despite his thirty plus years on earth. It was frankly perplexing and overly tiring to the older man. Lately, the balding man with the revoltingly full lips had been trying to tell him something, which McLean did *not* want to hear.

Deciding that he didn't want another uncomfortable scene, McLean steered his creaky body towards his favourite hiding place; the high balcony which ran uninterrupted around three sides of the church, just under the eaves. It was a good thinking spot and had been for the last twenty years although his muscles complained nowadays at the steep climb via the rickety back stairs and his heart fluttered dangerously for a while after the courageous ascent. As he peered down into the nave of his Lord's ancient house, the light stone reflecting the flicker of candles and tea lights, McLean saw his curate asleep on one of the pews in the south transept and sighed bitterly. He walked carefully around the walkway, his feet scuffing quietly along the worn stone until he had covered the remaining two sides of the cavernous space to where he could look down on his sleeping assistant. The overwhelming and unchristian urge to let a dob of spittle land on the lazy man's head, caused McLean an uncharacteristic moment of mirth and he clamped his age-spotted hand to his thin lips to prevent the abominable behaviour from taking form. Then a plan came to him and with a smile he scurried back towards the unlocked balcony door and the steep stairs.

He would ring the bishop himself before the counsellor did. And he would blame it all on Brian.

CHAPTER THREE

Jayden shook out her umbrella under the porch of the counselling rooms. Its cloth surface was still wet from her morning walk to work and she sincerely hoped that its sodden self would see her successfully home again. Droplets scattered all around her like light prisms of confetti and she hoisted it up over her head. She delicately picked her way through the crazy paved track around the outside of the building until it met the flying buttresses of the old church. It was an immense structure, constructed during the Norman conquest of Britain. Its history was colourful and varied, a rich tapestry of human involvement. The path meandered its way timelessly through the churchyard, which was recently valued at an incredible two million pounds-worth of prime central city real estate and disgorged Jayden onto the pavements of Lincoln High Street.

Outside the grounds came an immediate change in atmosphere. Shops and chain stores flogged their wares like beacons into the growing darkness and Jayden sighed and set off for home.

Her boots sloshed in the gathering puddles and the umbrella groaned under the weight of the January downpour but she battled on up the busy pedestrianised High Street, crossing Silver Street at the lights and emboldened by the fact that she didn't have far to go. She thought for a moment that she heard her name being called but it was indistinct and

Jayden dismissed it, pushing her hand deep into her handbag to retrieve her front door key.

A sudden grip on her forearm made her turn defensively and her eyes flashed dangerously. *Fear* settled on her head, obscuring rational thought and bringing a red veil down over her vision. It felt as though Jayden's heart halted in its business, resuming loudly in her chest as she recognised the face in front of hers.

"Sorry, sorry," the man said, raising his hands and jumping back from the can of pepper spray in Jayden's other hand. "Stupid of me in the dark, sorry." Strong arms pulled her into an embrace by way of apology, but it was not pleasant.

"Raff! You're soaked!" Jayden squeaked, fear leaking from her voice as she pushed him roughly away, shoving the mini aerosol back into her coat pocket and keeping her shaking hands busy to disguise her threatened petrification. Her friend looked chastened. She unlocked the front door and led the way inside, shutting and bolting it securely behind them. Jayden called it her 'magic door,' hidden between the bay windows of two of the larger shops on the High Street and consequently completely unnoticeable. The same colour as the brick work when closed, it entirely disappeared from view leaving only the four steps up to the entrance.

The street was narrower and crowded with continuous buildings where Jayden's bolt hole lay and it suited her just fine. Nobody ever knocked on her door without texting first, her closest friends seeming to understand that she didn't open the door without warning. Not ever. In truth, she wouldn't hear knocking anyway, not as high as she was from the street. Her flat occupied two storeys of its own which included a spectacular roof garden and Jayden had deliberately ignored the need for the installation of a door bell, choosing to close the world out once her door was sealed shut. On the bottom two levels of the building a clothing store operated, touting its expensive wares to the city at large. Designer tracksuits and surf gear adorned the window display, not Jayden's usual fare at all. Despite living above the boutique, she had ironically never been in there for a look around, knowing that she would inevitably emerge empty handed. It wasn't in her nature to waste time. Not anymore.

Jayden pulled her wet boots off and stood them on newspaper at the bottom of a set of wooden stairs. Flicking the light switch with practiced fingers, she and Raff were bathed in a yellow glow and made their way up steep steps to the flat, two floors above. Turning sharply left at the top of the stairs took them into an open plan living area, occupying the whole upstairs floor of the shop beneath. Recently redecorated, the space was a neutral, muted area, offering gentle relaxation and safety, high above the activities of the franticly paced city. Enormous sash windows faced out onto the Victorian buildings opposite, their view obscured by red brick and the sightless eye sockets of office windows. Jayden dropped her handbag and keys onto a glass dining table whose perfect construction contrasted with the window panes adjacent to it, their surfaces betraying ancient, bubbled imperfections.

Walking towards the centre of the huge open space, Jayden disappeared up a spiral staircase to the floor above. Raff stood aimlessly as she went up it, her tight skirt swishing against her stockinged legs. After a moment's hesitation, he followed her. "Turn round!" she said to him crossly, emerging from an ensuite bathroom tying her long hair up into a ponytail. Raff turned his back on her, staring out through patio doors into the large, darkening rooftop courtyard which took up a third of the floor space. There were flowers blooming there despite the hard frosts and it looked neat and tidy. The windows of the second bedroom on the other side of the oasis glinted back at him through the foliage, lifeless and empty, it's sumptuous fittings unused as long as he had known their owner.

Raff surreptitiously watched Jayden's reflection as she moved around the bedroom, curious to see the movement of her long shapely legs, neat stomach and her improved muscle definition. He observed with a proud detachment, rather as an artist critiques his work from a distance to gain perspective, thinking; *I created that*. His dark hair cropped close to his head, he admired his reflection in the glass, relieved that his thirty-four years were wearing well on his toned, athletic body. Italian genetics winked back at him through olive skin and deep blue penetrating irises, in eyes that were dark-lashed and expressive.

Jayden laid her work clothes carelessly on the wide double bed and reached into her wardrobe for a pair of tracksuit pants and a comfortable tee shirt.

"No!" Raff demanded, turning quickly and catching her in her bra and knickers.

"I said turn around!" Jayden cried horrified, holding the tee shirt up to her chest in a defensive attempt to cover herself.

"Don't put those on," her friend begged. "I need

your help. Please put something decent on."

"No," Jayden sounded like a three-year-old. Raff groaned and in a fluid motion, crossed the room and ripped open the door of the pine wardrobe in frustration. He held up a glittering black cocktail dress victoriously.

"This! Wear this!"

Jayden stamped her foot crossly as Raff bent down and rummaged in the bottom of the wardrobe for matching shoes. The irony was not lost on her; that he was dictating her style of dress whilst wearing his work gear of gym branded tee shirt and shorts, which despite the cold weather, displayed his tanned hairy legs and muscular calves to perfection. He popped out of the wardrobe and stood up, his elegant face beatific with pleasure at the feel of the strappy sandals he clutched in his hands. "Weirdo," Jayden laughed at him. Raff's face crinkled pleasantly as he tipped his handsome face sideways at her and beamed. His straight, white teeth gave him the look of a model, striking Italian heritage oozing out of him in waves of testosterone.

"I worry about you, Mr Abbadeli," Jayden teased and Raff sniggered, but still kept hold of the shoes. "I don't want to go out, Raff; I've had a pig of a day..."

Her friend alarmed her by unexpectedly throwing himself on her plush double bed and burying his tousled head in his arms. Jayden pulled a distasteful grimace and hoped that he wasn't getting sweat all over her covers, before recommencing her dressing. Once the offending track pants and tee shirt were suitably covering her, she sat down on the bed and patted Raff's back as though he were a four-year-old and not a man of thirty-four. He sighed heavily and wiped his eyes dramatically with the back of his hand, unfortunately forgetting that he was still clutching the heel straps of the sandals and complaining when the leather caught his skin and the buckle produced a small nick on his cheek. He certainly whinged like the proverbial four-year-old.

Jayden lay on her back next to him and Raff laid his glossy dark locks on her stomach and snuggled in. She began to stroke his hair and pouted when his hair gel felt sticky under her fingers.

"Please help me?" Raff whinged.

"What does your surname mean?" Jayden asked curiously and Raff popped his head up surprised.

"Little priest in Italian," he said and then frowned angrily as Jayden laughed. His head bounced up and down on her stomach and coupled with the cross, petulant face he pulled, it only served to make her mirth even greater.

"It's not funny!" he growled annoyed when she only giggled harder.

"*Is* funny!" she shrieked.

In revenge, Raff began to tickle her and Jayden squealed, both hating and enjoying it at the same time. He tickled her until tears ran down her face, but when his fingers accidentally strayed to the ribs of her left side, she let out a groan of pain. "Sorry, sorry!" he exclaimed, pulling up her tee shirt and kissing the livid red scar that resided there, knowing that he was the only other person in the city who knew of its perfidious existence. He knew *of* it, but not *how* it had come to be there on her creamy lithe midriff.

"It's ok," Jayden pushed him roughly off her and sat up. But it wasn't ok and Raff knew that the fun was irrevocably over.

"Please help me?" he went back to whinging to distract her and Jayden smirked.

"As long as it doesn't involve me wearing those shoes or going back out in the cold," she replied, watching Raff's pleasant features cloud over in disappointment.

CHAPTER FOUR

Jayden's 'help' did not include the shoes in the end, but it did require better clothing and a trip out into the bracing winter evening. She moaned and grumbled the whole time as Raff chose her a pair of tight, black slacks, an appealingly fluffy, mauve pullover and permitted her to wear her long, black, high heeled boots. "It's cold," Jayden whinged as Raff bundled her up the road in a heavy overcoat and stuffed her inside his flash bottle-green Mercedes. He put the heated seats on and started the engine, still in his shorts and tee shirt and looking none the worse for wear. The car purred uphill, taking the myriad turns under ancient city gates which arched overhead, until it reached Raff's expensive house in the angular courtyard between two of the city's strongholds, church and state.

The house was an imposing structure which overlooked the top of iconic Steep Hill. At one end of the street stood the beautiful Lincoln Cathedral and at the other, Lincoln Castle. It was the location to die for and it hardly seemed to bother Raff that his Georgian townhouse was also one of the most photographed buildings in the city. It stood proudly, three stories high with a formidable roof balcony. The downstairs level housed a thriving antique business topped by a luxurious set of apartments upstairs. Raff's penthouse flat was plenty big enough for a very rich, unattached city businessman.

He dropped a grumpy Jayden off at the front step with a door key and the code for the burglar alarm. "Go in and put the kettle on, there's a love."

Raff's smart green saloon made a rumbling sound as he swung around on the cobbles and headed back down Drury Lane to a garage further down the hill, which he amiably rented for a small fortune.

Jayden sighed and pushed the key into the familiar lock, having done this drill a million times before. The house was empty and silent, but the central heating clicked comfortably in the gravity fed radiators, pumping hot water through the metal pipes and warming the huge house valiantly. Jayden bypassed the downstairs rooms belonging to the antique dealer and climbed the thickly carpeted treads, deactivating the alarm on the landing. The upstairs flat had been sumptuously decorated in period style, by far more expensive interior designers than Jayden would have aspired to be, had her life turned out differently. She stroked the textured wallpaper with gentle, seeking fingers, feeling as if she had no right to be there amongst the opulence.

As promised, Raff was quick, depositing the car and jogging up the hill. When he saw Jayden sitting in his kitchen still in her coat and boots nursing a large glass of Merlot, he made no comment, giving her boots the most cursory of disdainful glances. Jayden stuck her tongue out at him and dared him to make her take them off. He stole upstairs to the top floor to get a shower and change his clothes and Jayden followed him after relenting and obediently removing her boots and outer layers. She sat in the bathroom doorway on the carpet, her back leaning against the door jamb and sipped her wine. "What's for dinner then?" she called to him as water slopped and slapped the floor of the shower cubicle.

"Take away. Indian," he called back. Jayden wrinkled her nose and tried not to be churlish. She had made no secret of the fact that she didn't want to be here, especially not as a key actor in this ridiculous charade.

"Why's your brother coming down?" she asked.

"No idea, he rang a couple of hours ago and asked if he could stay."

"You don't need me," Jayden complained, "you should be honest with him. This is ridiculous! Don't you dare try and pretend I'm your girlfriend like you did with your parents, otherwise I'm going to embarrass you for sure."

Raff emerged from the bathroom with a towel wrapped around his waist. It left very little to the imagination as it only reached to his knees and clung to his powerful frame with the tiniest corner tucked in on itself. Jayden looked away and sulked. Raff nudged her with a wet toe and she grabbed at the towel mischievously. He laughed and skittered away. "I can't disappoint my parents again," he stated. "It didn't go so well for my brother."

"Is he gay too?" Jayden asked in surprise. Her friend had hardly mentioned his older brother in the last five years and it made her feel affronted on Raff's behalf, that he perhaps lived a lie because of a sibling's mistake. Raff poked his head around the doorframe, looking comical.

"No. He denounced the Catholic Church and Father went absolutely loco. Father's not a priest but he works for them in some capacity, as did his father and grandfather. We were brought up in such a strict

Catholic environment that it caused a massive ruckus. Father didn't speak to him for about four years. He took Mother and stomped back off to the Vatican for three of those."

"How old is your brother?" Jayden asked disinterestedly.

"Forty-two," Raff replied with a smirk at her feigned boredom.

"Are you close?"

Jayden's question came wistfully, as she strove vigorously to bury some deep hurt that threatened to bust open in her heart. Raff wished that she would level with him sometimes about her past. It was a sticking point in their friendship. Sometimes the spirit of *Fear* wafted around her like mist. "No. Not really. He was off and gone by the time I got rid of my acne and realised that I batted for the other team. Fortunately, he had already dropped his bombshell by the time I had gone off to university here. Otherwise, I would have been bound for Rome as well."

"I thought your parents were sweet," Jayden commented in a soft voice that was so laden with yearning, it tore at something in Raff's chest.

"They are. They just have high expectations of their sons."

Raff came out from behind the doorframe and dried his hair vigorously on the towel, scattering droplets like chicken feed. He seemed to have forgotten that he was stark naked as he recounted his family crisis and observed his friend, understanding her no better now than he had at the start. Then the moment dissipated like fog as Jayden ogled him shamelessly.

"You're a waste of a great body that's what you

are!" she pouted and Raff did a rude sign over his shoulder as he skittered back into the bedroom. Jayden smiled sadly to herself, affirming her oath to celibacy with a wistful force of will. It was one thing to look, but she knew that it was not for her. Not ever.

A dreadful thought occurred to her. "Please tell me you haven't invited Peter to this fake soiree?"

"As if!" came the instant retort. Jayden heaved a sigh of relief. The last thing she needed was a showdown with her best friend's *actual* partner, who hated her guts with an almost tangible passion. The problems had begun just over a year ago when Peter and Raff had first met. Peter's jealousy had been aroused almost immediately, possibly by the fact that Raff talked constantly about his friend, Jayden and Peter assumed that it was another guy. Then when they had been allowed to meet, put together tentatively like a couple of strange dogs and watched for signs of bared teeth and tail wagging, Peter had been sharp and biting, visibly irritated by Raff's easy physical contact with his female friend.

Raphael Abbadeli made the perfect friend but even if he had been straight, he was still far too vain and self-obsessed to have interested Jayden, despite the fact that she had sworn off relationships for life. Unaware of either fact and consumed by his own inadequacy, Peter set out to humiliate her at every opportunity, turning his particular cutting brand of spite on her as often as possible. Consequently, Jayden avoided him like the black plague and Raff kept them apologetically apart. Jayden had cause to feel concerned for her friend as he recounted the dramatic stories of his boyfriend's temper tantrums, recently more frequent as Raff resisted the pressure for Peter to move in with him.

Jayden sat on the floor with her long legs tucked underneath her. She ran through the incident outside her front door, trying to compartmentalise it so as to deal with her old friend, *Terror*. It took constant effort to keep its influence from dogging her emotions and Jayden worked on her rational mind, reassuring herself that she was safe, both now and earlier. Raff was no threat to her.

As a bachelor, Raff was hot property, whatever his predilection. As the owner of a successful gym which he still ran himself each day, he was worth a fortune, hence the expensive piece of real estate at the top of the heart attack inducing hill.

At the age of thirty-four, he had still not confessed his sexual preferences to his crinkly brown elderly parents or his brother, the latter of whom Jayden had not yet met. Despite living a life that was outside the bounds of biblical acceptance, Raff was surprisingly old fashioned and it continually made Jayden smile. A Christian herself, Jayden detested the sin, whilst shamelessly adoring the sinner and it was another area of contention between her and Peter as the other man strongly desired to use her faith against her in her relationship with Raff. He had once been forced to apologise to her grudgingly, for accusing her of not being a 'proper' Christian because of her affection for Raff. It seemed that her faith precluded that such friendships must not exist, in the world according to Peter. Jayden suspected that Peter was something of a latterly insolvent gold-digger and also that he was quickly wearing out his welcome with Raff.

Jayden helped Raff make up one of the sumptuous

spare rooms on the top floor above the living areas. Raff had arrived in the city five years before Jayden's enrolment at the university, waving a wad of cash from inheritance money and a great business plan. He had completed a three-year sports science and management degree and two years after that; he was the owner of the *'Fat Lads and Lasses'* gym and the house at the top of the hill. Jayden had only met him five years ago when she entered his gym on a trial visit, looking for a way to rid herself of the excess few pounds from poor university-student dietary habits.

Raff had made up her exercise plan which he strictly forced her to adhere to three times a week even now, changing it up periodically to make her grumpy and out of sorts. Although he was attentive to all his clients, he had taken a particular shine to Jayden and their interesting friendship was launched. What was different about his gym, was that he kept the sexes strictly apart, working on the philosophy that nothing useful gets done when there are posers around. Consequently, he had the 'fat lasses' upstairs working away without self-consciousness and the serious male gym-goers downstairs with all the other 'fat lads.' Somehow it worked and made money. Lots of money.

A knock on the front door heralded the arrival of Raff's brother. Jayden waited at the house while the men went and put the guest's transport away in the garage, although Jayden wondered how on earth they would fit another car in there with the Mercedes. The mystery was solved when Raff introduced his elder brother, clad head to foot in motorcycle gear.

Eduardo Abbadeli was as easy on the eye as his younger sibling. He was more slender in build and slightly taller, but no less handsome. In fact, they could almost have been twins but for the crow's feet at the outer corners of Eduardo's perceptive eyes and the peppering of grey at the fringes of his hair. The same dark locks and blue eyes shone out at Jayden as she shook his hand, but she felt instantly guilty when he produced a small brooch as a gift for her.

"Oh you didn't have to. But thank you." She didn't deserve it and glanced across at Raff with an unreadable look on her face.

As they reached the kitchen and Jayden began to open a bottle of white wine, the front door bell went again for the take out delivery and Raff dived off down the stairs. Ed sat at the table and ran his hands through his glossy hair, making it stick up at the front. He looked exhausted. "Tired?" Jayden asked him softly as she laid cutlery down in front of him. Ed politely thanked her and shifted so that she could set a water glass on the table next to his place. She caught a whiff of a masculine aftershave and liked it.

True to his word, Raff did nothing to infer that they were boyfriend and girlfriend, but unfortunately, Ed made his own assumptions. They ate companionably and chatted about current affairs and the state of the economy and the evening was going well. A couple of times Raff winked kindly across at Jayden, obviously pleased with how it was turning out. But then Ed took a phone call on his mobile phone, blocking one ear to the sound of voices and cutlery scraping across plates as his chair ground backwards on the glossy black and white tiles. He appeared disappointed when he returned to the kitchen and Jayden had purposefully overheard a muted conversation. "It can't be helped," Ed said in a low voice. "I'm really sorry my friend. Don't worry about anything, I'll take care of it."

All was well, until the next round of loud hammering sounded on the door.

Raff went back downstairs, resenting the notion that his quiet retreat had begun to resemble Piccadilly Circus. Even from the floor above, Jayden and Ed could hear the rancorous argument which rose loudly up the stairs. They both got to their feet, but the commotion reached the landing before they had gone very far from the spiced remains of their meal. Peter burst in through the doorway. "Oh, I might have guessed that you'd be *here!*" he snapped, on seeing Jayden. He turned angrily to face Raff. "Why do you always wheel *her* into your plans? For pities sake, leave the woman alone, why don't you? What is wrong with you?"

Embarrassment settled on the room like a stifling blanket, overheating everyone except Peter, who continued to rage on. Ed remained standing and looked enquiringly at his brother, asking wordlessly if he wanted him to intervene. Raff added his anger to the noise and the ready flow of testosterone sparked awful memories for Jayden, which spewed out into her inner vision like a video rerun. As *Terror* smirked happily and settled on her head, exacerbating her feelings of helplessness, she bolted.

The frightened woman reached the street without her coat or scarf, stuffing her feet into the long leather boots on the way out of the front door. The overwhelming fear engulfed her, holding her captive and it was a familiar and unwelcome sensation. Her demons caused her to flee without regard for her own safety in the darkness of the city, goading her on with snickered threats and memories of another, angry, persistent male. Once outside in the freezing night air, the influence of *Fear* grew, snaking around her shoulders with its scrawny withered arms as she faced the mile or so of lonely walking by herself. Raff had promised her a ride home and purposely not drunk any alcohol and so she had come out with only her phone and door key. She had no money for a taxi. Steep Hill loomed ahead of her, a dangerous, cobbled descent with shadowy corners into which she could be pulled and harmed.

Jayden steeled herself and decided to run home, figuring that it would be her safest option. She had just reached the sharply angled front window of the Reader's Rest bookshop when she heard someone coming after her and panicked.

"Wait up," it was an unfamiliar male voice, jangling her nerves and making her go quicker. But the descent was treacherous at the best of times and her speed was not helping. On a long straight part of the hill, Jayden felt herself losing control and she cannoned sideways into a guard rail, finding herself on her knees, her hands gripping the smooth, hand-worn metal awkwardly above her head.

Ed puffed up to her. "Didn't you hear me calling you?" He sounded cross but tenderly lent Jayden his hand, helping her up from the cold grey flags. Her bruised knee caps felt skinned and sore through the rough material of her slacks. For a moment, Jayden remained bent at the waist as though someone had cut her strings from above. It bought her a little time as the clock marched relentlessly by, surprised by how embarrassed she felt, going to pieces in the striking man's presence. Shaking hands rubbed at the knees of her trousers and her fingers found torn cloth. Sighing in irritation, Jayden stood up straight and braced herself for Ed's consternation. As the earth revolved nonchalantly, tethered to its predetermined axis, Jayden held her breath and waited, her rosebud lips pursed expectantly.

"Are you two-timing my brother?" Ed asked, his voice sounding roughly expelled from his lungs. It wasn't the question that Jayden had expected and her pretty face betrayed a stunning lack of guile as she frantically sought a suitable reply.

"No."

Surely honesty was the best policy. Ed's blue eyes narrowed and a flickering Victorian street lamp nearby caused his sapphire irises to dazzle and glimmer spectacularly. His head bounced just once on his neck, acceding albeit reluctantly, but he eyed Jayden with suspicion and something else which remained hidden from her. "I'll be fine from here," she stated, injecting a false calm into her voice and knowing even as she spoke the words that her enlarged pupils betrayed her fear of the darkened street.

"Don't be ridiculous!" Ed's words fuelled mixed emotions in the woman's heart, forcing rebellion to vie with reassurance. Seizing her cold and reluctant fingers in his warm, strong ones, he pulled her towards him and set off striding down the slippery cobbles.

A relentless drizzle spattered the world, carelessly speckling the earth with yet more of its generosity. It forced Jayden to cling to Ed's arm, dismayed to feel only a light shirt sleeve under her palms as the soles of her boots struggled with their greasy hold on the cobblestones. Their comical progress ended after only five minutes, arriving at Jayden's front door soaked through their clothing to the skin. Ed's muscular frame was given up by the saturated flimsiness of his white shirt as it clung to expanses of his chest and shoulders in an uncomfortable embrace. A mortifying moment of awkwardness punctuated the horrendous evening conclusively and Jayden entered her sanctuary with a wave and a grimace. "Thank you, for...taking care of me."

Ed kept his thoughts to himself, waving fecklessly with a hand dripping rainwater and setting off back up the hill at a jog. Jayden leaned her back against the inside of the front door and regretted her hasty exit, which had inadvertently left Raff alone with his furious partner. It delighted her inexplicably that Ed had chosen to ensure that she was safe at the expense of his own flesh and blood. As thoughts of Raff threaded through Jayden's brain, she bit back the bubbling irritation at his treatment of her. She seemed so easily displaced from 'friend' to 'prop' in his deceptive play act of a life and this was not the first time.

Only a hot shower eradicated the ice from her bones, but nothing would erase the disappointment of duplicity. Especially now that Raff's deception had resulted in Jayden looking like a serial fornicator. She snuggled down in her comfortable double bed, ruing the awful sensation of saturated hair and making pointless forays into the land of the healing slumber.

CHAPTER FIVE

Jayden put her key into the lock and turned it, feeling a peculiar sensation which caused the hairs on the nape of her neck to prickle in warning. It was a feeling she used to get when the girls at school had whispered about her behind their hands, their desire for gossip outweighing the need for decency or kindness.

Jayden turned, shaking off *Humiliation* and scanned the dark street, raking the passing faces for someone showing a particular interest in her. People dashed by, hardly noticing the woman in the dark coat, smothered in the shadows between two brightly lit stores. They bustled with purpose through the cold, eager to get home to warm, lit houses and the promise of dinner.

Jayden looked back to the lower slopes of the pedestrian walkway as it narrowed slightly, to navigate the ancient city walls which poked up like ramparts at the edges of the modern flagstones. The twenty-first century marched quickly past the roughened stone, originally laid by hand and crafted into incredible structures such as the ancient Stone Bow, the original gate into the city. The rushing Lincoln commuters merely bobbed their heads in acknowledgement of its vital historical value, paying it scant lip service as long as no part of it impeded their progress.

Jayden sighed and pushed the front door open. Then it came again, that sixth sense warning her.

From her vantage point on the third step she swivelled her head and then she saw him. Down by the Stone Bow, whose gnarled and ancient bricks had slowed entry to the city for centuries as it glared down at the River Witham's murky depths, was the dark figure of a man. As her eyes settled on his face, she felt the breath go out of her in one terrifying gush of air and adrenaline took over, surging through her like acid, galvanising her and giving her options.

Part of the frightened woman wanted to hurl her bags to the ground and run after him, hit him and hit him until his pulped body slid into the dark river, erasing him from her life forever. But the bigger part, the sensible, rational part, urged her to go inside and slam the door against him. As her frantic eyes focused on him again, he turned and blended into the crowd like drifting fog and was gone from view. Jayden felt physically sick.

Realising her vulnerability abruptly, she kicked away envelopes littered on the floor behind the front door, where the postman had pushed them through the letterbox and spun around to close the door firmly behind her. She met resistance. At first, her brain told her that it was just the rug sticking, or the letters in the way, or something else that was making the door impossible to shut. But then *Fear* launched itself at her sense of reason and she let out a gasp of horror as she knew without a doubt, that somebody else was on the other side.

Jayden put her full weight behind and gave it a vicious shove, wanting with all her might to prevent that 'somebody' from gaining entrance and hurting her all over again. She heard herself cry out in anguish and a muffled sound erupt from the other side. Blood surged and pounded so loudly through her ears and brain that she was completely deaf and it wasn't until she heard her name being called that something snapped inside her head. The person on the other side was calling her new name, 'Jayden' not her old name. *Surely he couldn't possibly know that?*

Hesitation gave her opponent an opportunity and with a mighty shove, the door jabbed inwards and slammed Jayden back against the narrow hall wall. She was winded and terrified as the tall shape of a man entered her safe place. He was dressed from head to toe in black material which shone peculiarly in the glow of the street lamps outside. His head was completely covered and Jayden's breath came in snatches as she closed her eyes and slid down the wall. She had known this moment would come and there was a sense of peaceful acceptance that arrived with it. Not of welcome, but more a nodding acquaintance with her fate. "Jayden, I'm so sorry. I didn't mean to shove it that hard, but I could hear you calling out. I thought there was somebody in here with you and I...crap Jayd; I'm really sorry."

The man's voice didn't sound like *his*. It was deeper and more together. *Had she really been crying out?* Jayden concentrated on breathing and focused on the extraordinary fact that she wasn't going to die right then. It gave her such a feeling of relief that she cried loudly and unashamedly, tears dripping down her face and bouncing off the fluffy lapels of her coat. She heard the click of the front door and the clatter of the motorbike helmet being removed and set down on the red quarry tiles. Ed's muscular body sank down next to her and he placed an arm awkwardly around her shoulders, pulling her into him gently at first and then when she didn't resist, dragging her in more firmly.

He kept apologising. He said sorry close to forty times as they sat cuddled together on the cold floor tiles downstairs and another thirty once they had made it upstairs to the flat. Jayden said very little in response, allowing him to follow her upstairs and into the living room, but leaving him there to climb up to the next level, seeking solace in her bedroom. Once there, she stripped off her work clothes, discarding the smart grey suit over her bed and donning jeans and a comfy sweater. She examined her face in the mirror of the ensuite finding it blotchy and mottled from her extended bout of crying.

Jayden rinsed her cheeks with cold water and face-wash, drying roughly on an expensive maroon towel as if in punishment for her face's betrayal of her. Ample black eyelashes shrouded green eyes, which sought to protect and shield her from the world. Teardrops and water mingled on them, leaving tiny diamond-like sparkles as temporary disco decorations. She pulled her long curly hair free of its clips and let it hang down around her face and shoulders like protective curtains and ventured back out into the bedroom.

She was astounded to find her visitor waiting for her there and it gave her heart another little kick of fear. Ed stood by the bed looking utterly lost and a steaming mug of something teetered dangerously in his hand as he looked frantically for somewhere to put it. Jayden's eyes darkened as she felt incensed at the man's ignorant penetration of her safety. "You can't be here!" she exclaimed at him and his hand wobbled in surprise at the aggression in her voice.

Hot liquid slopped out of the mug and onto the wooden floorboards at his feet. He had managed to extract himself from his tight black leather motorbike gear and sturdy boots and seemed more rumpled in his jeans and white tee shirt. There was a large hole in the toe of his right sock and it made him appear deceptively vulnerable.

Jayden's brain shouted warnings at her which she frantically tried to process. She was a counsellor and dealt with people under stress every day of her working life. She understood better than most, the destructive patterns of behaviour that threatened victims of extreme trauma. She had done this so many times before, fought her demons with determination and courage and yet here they were again, laughing in her face with the same old tapes playing on repeat in her brain. With an exhausted sigh, she slumped down on the double bed and put her face in her hands.

Her hair moved slightly in the draught that Ed's movement caused as he gently put the dripping mug on the floorboards next to Jayden's foot. She heard the swish of denim as he went into the ensuite and returned with some toilet roll to mop up his spills. He was very close to her as he lifted the mug, wiped the bottom and then put it back down. His ministrations over, he seemed unsure what to do next. Making a decision, he sat down next to her on the bed without touching her and then to Jayden's great annoyance, flopped backwards across her bedspread.

Jayden glanced sideways at him, seeing how his tee shirt had come untucked from his denims. A black leather belt threaded through the loops on his jeans and a detailed buckle fastened at the centre. It had an attractive metal horse galloping across the leather, taking up almost the entire width of it. Jayden stared at it and wished that she was a horse, able just to run away. His stomach was brown and smooth, a snake of dark hair running from his belly button down into his jeans. An ugly appendectomy scar poked tantalisingly above the belt, an unfortunate crease of dented, stitched skin on an otherwise unblemished canvas.

"I need to make a phone call," Jayden said abruptly and, grabbing the mug of tea, made her way down the staircase to the floor below. Ed had brought her handbag upstairs and laid it on the dining table at the kitchen end of the room. With hands that shook a little less, Jayden found her mobile phone inside one of the pockets and dialled a number. "Hi, May," she said gently when the call was answered by a woman's lilting voice on the other end, "How is Mum today?"

The woman's reply seemed to bring comfort, even though she shouted slightly down the phone in a constant denial of her own deafness and as Jayden listened, her shoulders visibly relaxed and a grateful smile touched her pretty lips, turning her at once from defensive to beautiful.

"Hi Mum," Jayden intoned with tenderness as another wavering voice came down the phone in reply. "How are you today?" She nodded silently as her mother recounted her day, including all kinds of little details offered with a childlike enthusiasm. Jayden began to feel calmer at the sound of her mother's familiar voice. Hannah's gentle, lilting accent worked its way through her daughter's veins like a balm as she chatted about her trip to the beach yesterday and the ice cream that she and May had eaten on the promenade. Jayden was relieved for in those moments, she had her parent back and it was a blessed and precious tonic for the young woman. "Mum," she said quietly, "I think Nick might be out...Mum...Mum?"

She heard the clatter as the house phone hit the tiled floor of the old cottage in Aberystwyth. There came a cacophony of noises that caused Jayden to put the phone away from her ear in distaste. Then a disjointed, concerned voice came shouting back out of it. "Lily? Lily? Are you still there?"

Jayden put the phone back up to her ear. "Still here May. What happened?"

"I don't know my love, your mother just threw the phone on the floor and walked away. It's a shame. She's been so lucid today; I had begun to think that...never mind. It's just the way of this disease isn't it? Lulls us into a false sense of security and then breaks us down again."

May sighed heavily and Jayden could hear her heartbreak joining her own. "It's my fault. I'm sorry," Jayden breathed. "I asked about *him* and...well, I guess she doesn't want to hear it.

"Why did you mention your brother?" May asked and Jayden could hear the dismay and annoyance in her voice.

"I thought I saw him outside where I live," Jayden began and heard the sharp intake of breath cross the miles between her and her aunt. "I didn't know if the probation service had got in touch with you and let you know that he was out. They don't know where to find me..." The sentence tailed off as Jayden realised the futility of her situation. She was kicking herself. "I'm sorry. I shouldn't have asked Mum about him.

She just sounded so...normal. Do you think that maybe it's not Alzheimer's, but some complicated way of detaching after what happened?"

Hearing her aunt let out a snort of disdain, Jayden realised the unfairness of what she was asking. After all, it wasn't her who had to look after her mother was it? It was her poor aunt, trapped in the seaside town alone with someone who often didn't even know her. May had complained over the phone recently that Hannah could go to bed perfectly happy and lucid, kissing her sister goodnight and then waking up the next morning disoriented and afraid of the strange woman who was trying to help her get dressed. Jayden wasn't there was she? Guilt washed over the young woman like a wave, crashing over her soul as wickedly as the sea attacked the grey pebbles on the beach at Aberystwyth. What difference did it make what had caused her mother's disease? Knowing wouldn't make it go away.

"Nobody's called here," May was saying. "Surely he wouldn't try and find us, not after all these years?"

Jayden could hear the hope in her voice. They had all forged a life of sorts after her brother's wickedness had shattered their gentle family life and left his slug trail of misery coiling out behind him. May wanted to believe that they were all still safe, that the illusion of normality they had created for themselves was, in fact, real. Jayden didn't have the heart to disappoint her. "Of course he won't. I am sorry, May. It was stupid and thoughtless of me. Will you have a dreadful evening now?"

"No," May laughed. "She's got the snakes and ladders board out so I think she's probably forgotten already."

The momentary feeling of relief that Jayden instantly felt was smashed out of the way by the back draught of misery, which accompanied thoughts of her disappearing mother. As the phone call disconnected, she stood clutching the silent object in her hand and staring at the black screen, her face shrouded in the darkness which most of the time, she managed to keep hidden. The clearing of a male throat made her jump. *Ed*.

"You seem determined to give me heart failure tonight!" Jayden bit acerbically. He sat on the bottom step waiting for her to finish, his knees bent uncomfortably and his feet crossed, one over the other. His dark hair was sticking up at the front, making him look out of control. He also looked tired.

Ed pinched his nose between his thumb and finger hard as though stemming a headache and Jayden bit her lip. "Would you like some pain killers?"

He nodded and shifted himself off the step, hauling his body upright using the hand rail. Jayden went into the kitchen and reached up into a cupboard over the fridge to retrieve a packet of headache tablets. She popped two out onto the onyx black counter top and they skittered together near the sink. Retrieving a glass from a longer cupboard on the back wall, Jayden filled it from the tap and left it next to the tablets.

The kitchen wall had the distressed brick showing and it contrasted nicely with the black worktops and the pale grey cupboard fronts. An island faced the rest of the room, containing a sink and concealing a dishwasher and more cupboard space. It was formal and yet countrified, more of a bachelor pad than a sanctuary for a frightened woman. Ed pulled up a bar stool wordlessly and sat on the other side of the island, sipping the water and popping the tablets into his mouth both at once. Jayden felt suddenly awkward. Apart from Raff, she had rarely had other people in her home.

"It's a neat flat," Ed said smiling around. "You wouldn't know from the street that this exists. It's so hidden away."

Jayden smiled and nodded enthusiastically. "That's why it suits me. I feel safe here."

The slightest evidence of a frown crossed Ed's strong features as he considered the buried meaning in the words that the perplexing female opposite him had just uttered.

"Want some dinner?" Jayden's tone was rough and she looked genuinely surprised when he nodded, slowly at first but growing in momentum.

"I can nip up the road for some fish and chips," Ed offered, mortified when the shadow drifted instantly across Jayden's face. She shook her head, not wanting to open the front door again before she had to.

"No, I'll make us a Chilli con Carne. I've got some mince in the freezer."

Jayden reached down to a vegetable box nestled at the side of the island. Made from rough wood, possibly pallets, it was painted grey to match the kitchen. Someone had stencilled vegetables onto its lid and added the words 'Produce of the Garden.' Jayden seized some onions from its depths and a sharp knife from a drawer that slid silently open at her touch. Adding a chopping board, she plonked the items down in front of Ed and went through a sliding door into what looked like a laundry behind the kitchen. Evidently that was the location of the freezer, as she reappeared with a packet of frozen mince that she tossed into a microwave over the inset oven. "I love the lay-out of this flat," Ed commented as he commenced his onion chopping and Jayden smiled at his compliment.

"I was so lucky to find it."

The room behind the kitchen was long and thin and housed the washing machine, tumble dryer and numerous shelves with tins neatly lined up. A small window up high would offer light during the day but the darkness outside required use of the bright hundred watt light bulb in the centre of the area. There was even a tiny toilet cubicle slotted into the space nearest to the entry doors. Plasterboard walls and a sliding door made the toilet and sink units compact and kept them apart from the laundry equipment.

The room had been well done, practical and hidden behind the kitchen during the renovations, the sliding door almost unnoticeable due to its colour which matched the cupboards and opened to a push-touch action, negating the need for door handles. The whole panel could easily be mistaken for a wall. As Ed fetched a tin of tomatoes and another of mixed beans from inside, he was surprised to notice some fairly hefty bolts at the bottom and top of the door. He paused in concern and then shook his head, returning with the tins as though nothing was wrong, even though the practically invisible cupboard had all the hallmarks of a panic room.

Jayden cooked steadily and with confidence. It felt comforting to have somebody else to cook for instead of her usual fare for one, a single microwave meal or a toasted sandwich. She used the electric rice cooker to make a decent portion for them both and then set the dining table over by the window. "Where's your motorbike?" she asked Ed suddenly, pausing with two intricate crystal wine glasses in her hand.

"Outside your front door actually. I pulled it up practically on your doorstep. I didn't fancy leaving it up by the Stone Bow. I assumed there wouldn't be much left of it."

Jayden shook her head knowingly. "No, you're right. So you probably don't want wine then if you're driving?"

Ed opted for orange juice and they sipped their respective glasses whilst waiting for the food to finish cooking. Silence descended over them, but it wasn't one of those awkward moments, just companionable and easy. Ed looked at the beautiful woman in front of him. On the surface, she seemed capable and professional, fully in control of her world and collected. Yet the reality of Jayden was confusingly different, almost the exact opposite. The stunning mane hung almost to her waist. Escaping from its ponytail in a never ending war, it was a veritable sheet of dark curls that bounced and tossed when she walked or moved to stir the meat dish. But Ed had seen a naked fear in her appealing emerald eyes, a deeply hideous monster of anxiety that seemed capable of controlling her from the inside. Her seclusion and the bolts on the back of the laundry door told him that she felt hunted by someone or something and it intrigued him, whet his curious appetite in a way that he hadn't known for too long. Who was she and what was she afraid of?

From his vantage point on the stairs, he had sat

down early enough to hear part of the conversation and a woman's loud voice on the other end of the phone calling out the name, 'Lily.' He looked up at Jayden through his long eyelashes and liked the name. It suited her more than the boys' title she was saddled with. *Lily* fit her better somehow, a more appropriate floral tribute to a beautiful woman. "Who did you think I was?" he asked, trying hard to sound casual. "Before, when I was calling you and trying to push the door. Who did you *think* I was?"

Jayden was stirring the mince on the hob with her back to him and Ed saw her whole body stiffen. She resembled a piece of hard, brittle wood and one kick in the right place would snap her clean in half. It was painful to watch. He instantly regretted his question and generously released her from it. "Dinner smells gorgeous. We're a good team."

He saw her relax and the tension go out of her spine. She pulled herself up straighter, collected herself and turned around with a smile. "Yes, we are. Why did you come here anyway?"

She dished the rice and mince onto the plates carefully, displaying a perfectionist tendency in the way that she created a pit in the centre of the rice to prevent the mince from spilling unattractively down the side of it. Ed realised that he enjoyed watching her a little too much and looked away. "Raff asked me to. He was sorry about last night and as he was working a late shift, he wanted me to see if you were ok."

Jayden shrugged and brushed it off. "He worries too much. I'm perfectly fine, as you can see."

Ed wanted to say, *'But you're not, are you?'* yet some instinct made him keep the comment to himself. They tucked into their wholesome meal companionably, watching each other intently with stolen glances, each trying to work the other out and hone in on their agenda. But both were guarded enough to keep their private lives exactly that way - private. Jayden was curious about how Ed made a living but didn't want to ask. For some odd reason, she didn't want to reciprocate; to tell this strong capable man, that she spent her days dealing with the brokenness of the town, the adulterers, the gamblers, the sorry individuals accidentally addicted to pain killers or sleeping tablets, men and women addicted to porn or alcohol. It was a noble profession but it pained her to acknowledge that most of her clients attended St. Jude's Church. It soiled it somehow, muddied the beautiful belfry and the stained glass windows with the inadequacy of the 'real' body of Christ. It also inevitably led to questions that Jayden's confidentiality clause made impossible to answer. When she had asked Raff what his brother did, he had just winked at her and told her that she would like him. She did. But perhaps a little too much.

Ed washed the saucepans and reassembled the cleaned rice cooker while Jayden loaded the dishwasher. They made small talk but it was easy and she wondered how she had felt such irritation at the man the previous evening, when he had only tried to be considerate and help her home.

Downstairs at the street door, Jayden became nervous again with the prospect of the dark night outside and the silent High Street.

"Thanks for dinner," Ed said with a smile. He stepped over the threshold, listening to the snap of the lock and the sliding of at least two bolts along the wooden interior of the door. He stood on the steps for a moment before launching down to the street and retrieving his bike. He had expected an infringement notice pinned on it at least, but the night wardens - perhaps realising the sense in parking the bike outside the house rather than in the layby - had left it alone.

CHAPTER SIX

"Hey babe. What did you do with my fit brother then? He's still out. Or did you kick him swiftly into touch and he's off drowning his sorrows somewhere?" Raff accompanied his reverie with a giggle.

"He just left. He shouldn't be long."

Jayden sounded miserable and Raff knew better than to press her for information. "Hey," he began, "I'm really sorry about the other night. I shouldn't have asked you to play 'happy families' for my benefit. I had no idea that it would go so horribly wrong."

"It's ok," Jayden answered softly. "It was never going to end well."

"I was actually hoping that Ed might have broached it with you tonight and that you would put him straight...about us...well, me really. Don't suppose you did?"

"Raff!" Jayden was shocked. Why did people always think that they could include her in their manipulative little schemes? "No, surprisingly your name didn't come up - apart from as the reason that Ed called round. How little you must think of me if you believe that I'd betray you like that!" Jayden was just getting into her 'how-dare-you' speech when she heard her friend bleating down the phone.

"I'm sorry, I'm sorry. I'm just getting desperate. I have no idea how I'm going to break the news to Ed and my parents; that their futile hopes of me ever producing offspring are completely out of the question. Added to the fact that I bat for the other side altogether. I'm thirty-five this year and I know they're all looking at me expectantly. Gosh, what a mess!"

Jayden sat down on her plush leather sofa and with the wall mounted television on mute, began to flick through the channels looking for company. "So what you're actually saying, is that you wanted *me* to tell your brother you were gay?" she commented astutely. There was a poignant silence before Raff answered,

"Yeah."

"Look," Jayden offered, "the best I can do is sit with you while you tell him if you like. I'm offering moral support, but that's all. Apart from mopping up the tears or blood afterwards, you have to do the hard part yourself. It's only right."

"I know," Raff sighed. "I've just left it so long that it gets more impossible each year. Anyway," he brightened suddenly, "there won't be blood. Ed won't hit me. He hates violence. His sweetheart wouldn't allow it."

"Oh," Jayden was surprised by the disappointment that she heard in her own voice. "Ed's got a girlfriend or...married?"

On the other end of the call, Raff hooted with laughter.

"Married, definitely married. Not just the ball and chain, it's the whole bloody castle he's attached to! That's why it's going to be so hard to tell him about...what I am. He thinks marriage is the only way to go and he's going to hate me."

"It might not be as bad as you think," Jayden

comforted. "But the offer's there if you want it. I can be with you if you like."

Raff went back to sighing and thanked her. Before he rang off, Jayden begged him for a recap of the self-defence classes he had given her five years previously. "Why? What's happened?" he asked her sharply and she dismissed his concern with practiced ease.

"Nothing, I just feel a bit rusty. A woman went loco in an appointment yesterday and reminded me that I hadn't been practicing enough recently."

"Oh, ok." Raff calmed down and arranged to meet her at the gym after her last session the next day. "I'm on a late shift so we can eat afterwards if you like?"

Jayden rang off feeling easier about things. Raff had promised that his horrid boyfriend would not be there and that he would give Jayden a good work out. She looked forward to the physical activity and then the peace and calm of the weekend. She made herself a cup of tea and turned out the lights on the lower level before climbing the wooden spiral staircase up to her bedroom. There was no need to shut the curtains, as her floor length windows only opened onto the roof garden and nobody but passing aeroplanes would be able to spy in.

Leaving a lamp on in her bedroom, Jayden opened up the double doors and went outside in her slippers. The rain had stopped, leaving a glossy sheen on the paving stones around the edge of the roof garden. Walking over to the balustrade she leaned over, peering down into the dark street three floors below. A couple wound their merry way home, slightly drunk as they weaved across the street and back again. They made their way slowly up the flagstones towards Clasketgate until Jayden could no longer see the tops of their heads anymore.

The last five years had been filled with Jayden's unusual hobby, people-watching from her perch high above the heads of the great unwashed masses. She had seen fights, arguments, make ups and break ups, all from her detached vantage point. It suited her and *Loneliness* was a far better companion than *Fear*, she had decided long ago. Jayden sipped her tea and admired the stars overhead, glinting happily now that their cloudy shroud had been pulled off. If she leaned quite far out, she could just about see the dark grey of the Stone Bow in the distance, guarding the city from an ancient unknown foe as if someone had forgotten to tell it that there was no longer any need for its vigilance. The city was already overrun and hope was lost.

Lincoln had spewed beyond the safety of its gates for miles and miles in every direction. Like so many of the remnants of former strongholds, the ancient stone pile was now just a tourist attraction, something navigated with arms full of shopping and nagging children, photographed by fascinated newcomers and ignored by locals. Its history and its secrets cried out to Jayden and her heart responded, likewise. "We all have secrets," she said out loud to herself, moving across to the raised veggie garden on the back wall. Behind the wall was the staircase down from the bedrooms to the living area and a passageway went left and right from it. Left at the top of the stairs went to Jayden's bedroom, a huge room by any standards. To the right went to the spare bedroom, nestled on top of the roof, a smaller replica of hers.

It had been intended for Jayden's mother, Hannah, but her illness had prevented her from ever moving in. Hannah herself had chosen to have it painted in dusky rose pink, with cream bedspread and curtains. She would have loved it. Even the towels in the ensuite were a matching pink, soap all ready, but unused in a floral dish that had belonged to her grandmother. Once a week, Jayden dusted and cleaned regardless and remembered all that she had lost. Hannah had helped her to pick the flat, pandering to Jayden's need to remain invisible and unreachable, but a year later, would have struggled to find it again or even recall which city it was in. Hannah had generously released her late husband's trust fund for his daughter, so that Jayden had already paid off the remaining mortgage within the first four years. Sadly Hannah could no longer remember her soul mate's name anymore, least of all how he might have died.

Jayden snapped off some basil leaves and lifted them to her nose, savouring the childhood scent. The cottage garden in the wilds of Yorkshire had been home for her and she deliberately invoked happy memories with the things she grew in her garden. A small crop of potatoes nestled inside a sack, protected from the hard frosts by the height above ground level and the wrapping, creating newness in the folds of the soil. Pots of herbs were dotted around the patio area which was neat and perfectly aligned. It was Jayden's passion, investing hours into the little area above ground as though it was her secret garden. Because it was. It was both hers and secret. No-one tramping the cobbled streets of the city would ever have guessed that a veritable oasis grew above their heads. Only the view from one part of the castle ramparts gave it away in a 'wow' moment through the binoculars that tourists had to pay fifty pence to look through, but they would never be able to find it again from ground level. Not enough to point upwards and declare, 'there it is.'

There was no lawn although ironically, it probably would have grown well. Practical paving slabs decorated the area which occupied a third of the surface of the bedroom level. As a central city garden, it was enormous, bigger than some houses commanded on the ground but for a roof garden, it was spectacular. The ceiling of the living area had needed to be specially braced in order to add an upper level. Jayden had seen the architect's plans. It had been an immense project.

The businessman who had commissioned the conversion of the upstairs of the store had never lived in it. He had intended to but been head hunted for an executive job in America. Initially agreeing to lease the flat to Jayden and her mother for six months, he had gotten in touch via the rental agent soon after the contract was signed and expressed his desire to sell. Faced with the prospect of another difficult search, Jayden had bought it and never regretted the decision.

Fingering the delicate leaves of a weeping willow which spent its life in an enormous pot over by her mother's room, Jayden contemplated her life. It wasn't so bad. She had salvaged a huge amount from the spoils. It certainly could have been worse. The winter had stripped most of the leaves from the willow, but it remained in a permanent state of confusion. Unlike most trees down below, it lived in a peculiar microclimate. The wind only ever attacked from one side, occasionally coming in an unexpected direction and sneaking in over the balustrade from the street. Although it got cold on the roof, frost could not touch it and any daytime sunshine bathed it as if by right. The willow grew all year round, never knowing when it was time to stop, shed its leaves and rest. Even in January, in its state of continual flux, the little tree still had leaves and was growing.

Willows were Hannah's favourite and this specimen was purchased at a time when Jayden still hoped that she might at least come to stay. It would have been a perfect solution, respite for May, the loyal sister who had taken her into her own Welsh home and for Hannah, who wouldn't feel like a burden for a few days at least. Raff had carried the tree up the stairs and hefted up the giant pot afterwards with much grunting and complaint. He had managed to spill potting mix all up the first lot of stairs and they had giggled and swept it off with a dustpan and brush.

But Hannah's condition left her trapped in Aberystwyth and she had never seen her gift, despite the fact that it grew and grew faithfully in anticipation of the gleeful clap of her hands when she saw it. It had grown so big in just a few years that it wouldn't even go back through the flat anymore. It would need to be butchered and thrown over the balustrade into the street when its days were over. Jayden closed her eyes and ran her hand through the remaining leaves, hearing their papery noise and delicate brush strokes across her palms as she prayed for her mother with all her heart.

The edge of the roof above came out over the garden, half a metre on all three sides of the outdoor space and allowed for some shelter even in bad weather. Tiny spotlights had been fixed into the overhang all around, pointing downwards and adding a comforting glow. Jayden turned them on as she got into bed and read a novel to herself as she waited for sleep to visit. Some nights were harder than others.

Her thoughts wandered momentarily to Ed, admiring his strong physique and how much she had enjoyed the safety of his arms around her. For just a second, she felt regret that he was married and out of bounds, chiding herself with the ridiculousness of the notion. The only other male to have touched her since the attack had been Raff and that was because she was in no possible danger from him. Ed's arms had felt good and reminded her bizarrely of the strength in her father's embrace. Dan had been a great father. The best kind of father.

At the thought of his gentle, kind face, Jayden felt sleep running from her as a wave of *Guilt's* ugly influence tried to descend on her shoulders, vice-like fingers clawing at her flesh. With a practiced force of will, she pushed it away and it was a reflex action of the mind. She set the familiar tape playing in her brain.

I was not to blame. My father loved me. I was not to blame. Sometimes bad things happen. I was not to blame.

Jayden relaxed and used her breathing exercises to calm herself. The counsellor counselled herself in the same way she did others, five days a week. That's why she was so good at it. Because she understood from bitter experience, that it worked.

Jayden awoke the next morning feeling decidedly 'off' as her mother would have said. The spotlights which shone into the garden only highlighted the darkness of the northern hemisphere, which would stay black until after seven thirty. Jayden yawned and snuggled further down into her warm duvet, stretching out her legs in the large double bed. The sound of snuffling made her smile as the ginger Abyssinian cat poked her fluffy head up from the bottom of the bed and yawned in response. Nahla had woken Jayden at two o'clock, pounding her lithe pink paws on the bedroom door to come in out of the cold. She had been out on the prowl for hours, refusing to respond to her owner's whispered call as she had settled down for the night, instead chasing tiny mice in the roof guttering of adjacent buildings. Luckily Jayden had managed to get her in without the little grey tailed offering that Nahla had laid down on the doormat. "Naughty girl. You should have come in earlier," Jayden moaned to her and the cat stalked up the bed and began patting her on the forehead with soft, tender paws which in milliseconds could inflict awful injury on her mistress, but never would.

Nahla hated the busy street and the impatient cars at either end of the pedestrian walkway. She preferred to use the gable ends and the world of the roof dwellers to move around in, never venturing any further down than she had to. Her life's purpose centred on ridding the entire length of this side of the street of vermin. Occasionally when Jayden came home and looked up, she would spot the slender ginger frame perched regally on an upstairs windowsill down the street with no visible means of having got there. It had caused great concern initially and Jayden on a number of occasions had wondered whether the fire brigade would need calling. But Nahla always turned up at the bedroom door looking none the worse for wear.

Owning a cat in the middle of the city had seemed like a stupid idea, only properly thought through once

Jayden had already brought her home. The ticked ginger female was extremely rare as it turned out, due to the recessive gene which made little orange females uncommon. She was striped only on her legs and tail, the rest of her covered in an unusual patina of orange colouring, white at the roots and ginger on top. She had been the only kitten left in the shop. The owner had told Jayden sadly that people no longer liked 'gingers' and the prejudice had picked at some inner scale of justice in her.

In fear for Nahla's safety, Jayden had kept her new kitten indoors for six months frightened that she would get run over outside, trodden on or abused in some other way by passing drunks. But Nahla hated people and woe betide anyone who approached her when she was not in the mood to permit it. She tolerated Raff but hissed vehemently at other rare visitors and made a bee-line for an exit point. The only person for whom she was still a cuddly, playful kitten, was Jayden. Nahla was four years old but for her mistress, she was still a ginger ball of fun that would pop out from under curtains or beds unexpectedly and tag her calves with soft paws, thoroughly enjoying the ensuing squeals of shock.

Nahla rubbed her whole body along Jayden's face, causing her to cough and splutter at the fluffy ginger hairs that stuck to her nose and lips. The cat rolled onto her back and stuck all four legs in the air, but Jayden knew better. "You just want me to tickle your tummy and then you'll scratch me. I'm not playing today."

Jayden hoisted herself reluctantly up onto her elbows and looked out at the darkness beyond the glass. It did not look inviting in the pre-dawn glow, but there was a freshness in the air that hadn't been there the previous day. Her night had brought little rest. Instead of being unwelcome, Nahla's disturbance was a relief, waking Jayden from a dreadful dream. Nick's disembodied face had hovered at the end of her bed, pleading with her and begging her for help. His thick, brown hair hung greasy and straggly around his sweating face and his eyes were dark and listless. The addict's face twitched involuntarily and *Evil* flitted around the room as he writhed in discomfort, the drug leaking out of his body and leaving him empty and desperate. *"You have to help me, Lily. I've nobody left to ask. Don't make me beg. Don't make me hurt you."*

Seventeen year old Lily McGowan had shaken her head and refused. She had seen her brother's friends. They were petty criminals who made her feel ill and uncomfortable in their presence, especially Wes, Nick's newest buddy. There was something distinctly unhinged about him.

Nahla had padded against the door in the dead of night, proud of the dead mouse dangling from her front teeth and had inadvertently rescued her mistress from a terrible fate. If only the reality all those years ago had been so easily prevented.

Jayden shook herself and the cat jumped off the duvet and padded confidently to the top of the stairs, sure that 'feed the cat' would be top of her grateful mistress's list. By the time Jayden was ready for work, the weather had declared its intentions and the dreary, rain-soaked clouds had cleared, leaving a cold, blue sky.

CHAPTER SEVEN

"Cold enough to snow!" the vicar exclaimed as he rubbed his hands together to keep warm. The reception area always took a while to warm up. The ugly extension which had been slapped onto the back of the beautiful church was both an embarrassment and an eyesore. It was incredible what the 1970's had permitted. It also leaked like a sieve and let out heat in an attempt to bless the rest of downhill Lincoln. It was often warmer in the large, open plan department stores further into town than in the church's administration block.

"It'll warm up," Jayden reassured him, smiling as she unlocked her office. The vicar surprised her by following her inside and closing the door.

"About the other day," he began, "you're right. I shouldn't have inconvenienced you that way and I apologise. I fear that I am a little overwhelmed by today's problems and have spoken to the acting bishop myself. I rang him after you left. I've been resisting the diocesan's attempts to give me another curate for some time now, but I actually think that it'll be a good idea. He's sending this jolly chap down for me to have a look at and I hope that we'll rub along quite nicely."

He hopped from foot to foot and looked openly for Jayden's approval. She turned her hundred watt beam on him, flashing her perfect teeth and the vicar looked both relieved and gratified. Jayden contemplated apologising in return for the sharp way in which she had spoken to the elderly servant of the Lord, but experience told her to wait just a heartbeat before doing so. She was not disappointed. "Right then," the reverend intoned, "I'll check this chappie out. He won't formally start until next week so you and Cam will deal with all the difficult ones I can't seem to get through. I don't know what people are playing at nowadays. Pregnant fourteen-year-olds like that one the other day. She needed a slapped backside and locking in her room, not counselling. The vicar I worked for as a new curate wouldn't have stood for it. She would have been shamed at the front of the church and the parents...well, they have to take responsibility at some point! Dumping their problems on the church just isn't good enough."

Slamming the interconnecting door between the main corridor of the church and the admin block, the vicar flounced away leaving Jayden sighing heavily and feeling relieved that it was almost the weekend. She tried not to distract herself with the image of the girl's parents, ashen and shocked at what had happened to their little girl. Oh, they would take responsibility all right, tied down with a grandchild in their late thirties whilst watching their promising academic pour her life down the toilet for a few years. They didn't need McLean's caustic words as punishment, not on top of everything else they were trying to cope with.

Two alcoholics, one poor husband addicted to porn and a widowed middle-aged parishioner suffering from debilitating bouts of anxiety later and Jayden was ready to leave for the day. An external supervisor had sat in on her third session, using the hour afterwards to give her helpful pointers and allow Jayden to download some of her own misgivings and issues. It was all part of the process, the counsellors counselling the counsellors. Rita had been supervising Jayden for the past five years, ever since she had taken up the role at St. Jude's and had lectured at the university prior to that. The very capable psychologist had overseen Jayden's three-year counselling degree. There was an air of trust between the women, helped considerably by the fact that Jayden had been able to be completely honest with the older woman about her own demons. It had been pointless hiding them from her and besides, most of them had been dealt with in the openness of her degree. It had been the most healing course that Jayden could ever have considered doing and she fell into it, purely by chance.

After her brother's betrayal, Jayden had spent time with counsellors provided by Victim Support. She had been damaged and yet open about her needs and one of them had approached her and made the ludicrous suggestion that perhaps she might turn her experiences into a positive balm for others. Still grief-stricken by the tragic death of her father, Jayden had been reluctant but found a certain peace in the suggestion. At the end of her schooling, she had applied to Lincoln University and got in. Receiving an astoundingly good degree, first-class honours no less, Jayden had secured a job at the church and shackled herself more or less permanently to the city. Tired of halls of residence and flatting with animals disguised as students, Jayden had found her flat and made her plans, coping when Hannah's health declined so quickly that they were all dashed wickedly to the rocks. Rita knew it all.

"I thought it was him and I freaked out a little," Jayden told Rita as they chatted over coffee. Rita nodded encouragingly and made notes on her pad that appeared as little shorthand squiggles on the crisp white page. It was part of the drill.

There was always a risk with someone who had suffered their own trauma that it would affect their dealings with another hurting person. They could either transfer their experiences onto that person or absorb the client's hurts to a detrimental degree. They could judge the client, or shut down altogether. The aim of supervision was to provide checks and balances, to ensure that neither the client nor the counsellor suffered as a result of undealt-with issues, which had the potential to derail even the best treatment plans.

"How long did your brother get in prison?" Rita asked gently, watching Jayden for the familiar stress-tells whilst knowing that the other woman was perfectly capable of masking them if she chose to. Jayden's face remained neutral and her body relaxed as she answered.

"He got ten years. But I guess he could be out now, on probation."

"It was always a possibility that he might come looking for you..."

"But I thought I had covered my tracks," Jayden interrupted and Rita observed her carefully. "I changed city; I took a different name. I don't know what more I could have done." She was aware of her hysteria bubbling just beneath the surface and knew that Rita was too. "I'm fine," she said, collecting herself and sighing out slowly, "It can't have been Nick. It was just a shock that's all."

"How did the thought that he had found you, make you feel?" Rita asked, peering over her bifocals.

Jayden bit her bottom lip on the inside, thinking hard. "Angry, it made me feel scared but then angry. Like...really steaming angry."

Rita smiled. "So what does that tell you?"

In her head, Jayden flipped through her mental notes as she would for any client sat in front of her. Anger indicated a blocked goal, externally prevented by someone or something else. She backtracked through the five circles which she had roughly drawn, deep inside the workings of her brain and thought about her rational and volitional mind and the tapes that it played to her. It leaped out at her, as familiar as an unwelcome house guest whom you find it impossible to say 'no' to.

I must stay safe. I must stay safe. I must stay safe...

The person who either was Nick or who just resembled him, had challenged and destroyed that goal. *I must stay safe* had become, *I can't stay safe*, causing anger and self-recrimination. It was a stupid, unrealistic goal and always had been. Jayden was aware that she had absolutely no control over someone else's actions. It wasn't down to her to be responsible for her own safety and the burden had become unwieldy and impossible. All she could do was exercise common sense and hand the rest over to a higher power. Jayden flawlessly changed her tape and the anger dissipated almost immediately.

I am a child of God, he is more than able to keep me safe.

Jayden refused to listen to *Satan's* lies as he whispered how God hadn't done a very good job when she was seventeen, because if none of it had happened, she wouldn't be the person she was now.

She liked who she was and acknowledged it inwardly, as Rita sat and scribbled on her pad. But the line of 'ifs' rolled out before her like a blood red carpet at an award ceremony, demanding that she walk its crimson pile.

If Nick hadn't taken her from the house by force, bundling her into his mate's car and trading her to Wes for a cocaine hit. *If* her father hadn't seen him from the hill where he had been checking the sheep, he wouldn't have followed them to the dreadful squat in the centre of Bradford. *If* Dan hadn't been willing to wade in to save his daughter from his son's awful betrayal, he would never have been stabbed. *If* Dan hadn't died, Hannah might not be sick.

But if none of that had happened, she reassured herself, *I wouldn't be me.* She would be Lily, probably pursuing some different life elsewhere, working for an interior design firm perhaps and plumping cushions at some lonely rich woman's house. She wouldn't have the skills she had now which made the difference in a marriage, in a desperate person's life, in the changing of an adult's perception about themselves. She wouldn't be making the kind of transformations that she was now helping to forge and that was all *because* of her experience. Dan had shown his daughter that she was worth dying for and Jayden was not prepared to dishonour his memory by doing nothing with her life. She was going to love people, *whether they wanted it or not.*

Having found her equilibrium again, Jayden visibly relaxed and so did Rita. The spirits hovered nearby, *Fear* and *Self-doubt* waiting for their moment to descend again into her headspace. It would come. It always did. Familiarity gave them right of entry.

"My friend is going to give me some self-defence refresher lessons," Jayden told her supervisor, "partly just in case and partly to help me feel that I am in control of my life, not my life in control of me."

Rita nodded with approval. Her bright orange hair was coiffed in a high style which barely moved in the breeze from the heat pump, testament to her skill with hair spray. They chatted for a while longer until the knock on the door heralded the arrival of Jayden's last appointment for the day, the gentle widow who was valiantly battling the pressure of Agoraphobia in her lonely twilight years.

The self-defence lessons went predominantly well. Jayden had forgotten nothing, fuelled by a frantic need for safety, rather than a whim or desire for physical activity. Her skill was accurate and confident, proved by a rather effective kick straight into Raff's privates, leaving him rolling around on the wrestling mat for quite some time. Jayden was mortified as the tears streamed helplessly down the grown man's face and plopped off the end of his nose onto the squishy blue fabric. "Just do that. You'll be fine," Raff grunted, still curled into a ball, face down, gripping his manhood in a clenched fist. "I'll just put a sign on your back saying, 'Don't even bother' and a photo of me like this."

"Yeah." Jayden plonked herself down with a thud on the mat next to her friend and patted his back affectionately, her brain working through myriad scenarios. Raff sat up on his hairy knees, leaning back against the heels of his trainers and wiped his face with the bottom of his red tee shirt.

"What's wrong Jay?" he asked her, noting with satisfaction how her unguarded face betrayed her with the unexpectedness of his question. The screen came crashing down over her emotions with a second's delay. Jayden's eyes danced as she focused on different things around the gym, distracting herself from the answer she would not give. Three women walked on treadmills, chatting, laughing and waving their arms as they strolled, knowing that Raff was otherwise engaged and wouldn't be chasing them to put some effort in for a moment.

Jayden watched with the subtlest smirk on her full lips as Raff's assistant approached the women from behind, his red tee shirt and shorts rustling gently against his tank body. They jumped in unison like a disjointed Mexican wave as he spoke to them and each guiltily turned up the pace on their machines. Fat lasses were not allowed to remain so at the Abbadeli gym. "When I'm here with you practicing, I know it all and I can defend myself just fine. But in the dark on my way home, it's a different matter. I go to pieces and can't remember what to do. I'm useless."

Jayden's idle, nervous fingers sought a hanging thread which hung tantalisingly from the side of her trainers. She trapped it between thumb and forefinger and began to pull. Raff slapped her hand. "I bought you those!" he was indignant. "They weren't cheap, woman!"

Jayden mouthed a 'sorry' through pursed lips and Raff shuffled around so that he could wrap her in his muscular arms. The curve of his biceps acted as a firm pillow for Jayden's soft cheek and she closed her eyes and enjoyed the safety that proximity with this strong male offered, albeit momentarily.

"Er, hi." Ed's voice sounded awkward and Raff and Jayden pulled hurriedly apart, her brushing a hand across her eyes to dismiss the threatening tears. He was wearing an aged pair of shorts which had spots of white paint spattered down the side of the left leg and an old white tee shirt. He addressed his brother. "I just paid for a two-week membership, hope that was ok. I need to do some more work on my weights."

Raff jumped up in one fluid movement and Jayden was left sat on the floor, embarrassed. "It's fine and you didn't have to pay. Help yourself brother, what's mine is yours."

Raff gripped his sibling's upper arm and led him across to the weights area, thrilled to be interacting with him on home turf. It seemed to enthuse him with an infectious vitality that could be loosely labelled as 'showing off.' Jayden watched him, pleased and gratified for her friend's opportunity to finally shine. She gathered her sports gear together and quietly left. By the time Raff had finished pointlessly demonstrating the nuances of his expensive equipment to his childhood hero, he remembered his client and returned to the mat, disappointed to find that she was long gone. Jayden was already marching quickly through the darkness home, fists at the ready with renewed determination.

"Yuk!" The microwaved meal was insubstantial and tasted bizarrely of the container that it was cooked in. Jayden pulled her legs up onto the sofa and contemplated the uneaten contents of the white tray. It had claimed to be macaroni cheese but was clearly plasterboard with essence of fake cheese substitute doused with pepper. In misery, she got up and slung the offending object in the dustbin under the sink, placing the metal fork in the dishwasher.

Numerous stylish bookshelves lined the living

room end of the floor. Jayden's passion was books and she had made no apology for the purpose built shelving. She was compulsive about neatness and so her books were all in height order on their shelves, neatly regimental like a small paper army. She fingered the collection of dust covers, settling eventually on an elderly copy of Daniel Defoe's *Roxana*. Inset lights cast a soft glow over the spines of the various manuscript soldiers standing at attention and Jayden turned off the overhead lights and snuggled down in an antique chaise longue.

She had read the book a million times already and found it humorous and calming. Defoe was a man who wrote in 1600's England purely for the sport of it, an opportunist who unashamedly made money from his craft and yet spent his entire life in debt. Pilloried for offending the authorities, Defoe wrote a poem about being in the stocks called *Hymn to the Pillory* and paid a small child to sell it to onlookers for him. Legend told that instead of rotten food; the townsfolk threw flowers instead. It was the character of the man who attracted Jayden, the unstoppable verve of his thirst for life.

Yet even Defoe's energy had come to a grinding halt. He was reported as dying whilst in hiding from his ever persistent creditors, but the lesser known truth was that he had died of lethargy. It was a thought that had tortured Jayden as she tried to recover from the attack that had robbed her of both her spleen and her father. She had pondered then on what it must be like to allow your body just to remain still until all energy and its will to live had drained completely from it. The long nights in the hospital had given her an insight far beyond her years and she clung to the battered book now, in fingers that had retrieved their purpose in life from the brink of the nothingness.

Unable to fully settle, Jayden sniffed at the comforting musty smell of the book, running the spine along the end of her nose like a small child with a favourite blanket. A friendly meow came from the kitchen as Nahla enjoyed her night time kibbles and padded across on tiny pink paws for a cuddle. Friday for Jayden ended early with a shower, a small, sprightly ginger cat and a very old book, safely cosseted upstairs in the wide, squashy bed. Her phone stayed on the work surface in the Spartan kitchen and so she failed to hear the text that bleeped once and then fell silent, or the knocking of the worried brothers on her street door some time later.

Sometimes people shrouded themselves in isolation, as a protective blanket from potential hurt and inadvertently removed themselves from the blessing that interaction brought. They caused the thing they dreaded. Jayden knew all that. She spent each day calmly guiding other damaged souls to a lightness of being, but failed dismally at her own deeper healing.

Nahla wittered and grumbled until Jayden allowed her inside the covers and then she settled near the footboard and cozied down, her delicately furry body nestled next to Jayden's toes. In her own way, she offered the most ancient form of comfort to her human being, that which had originated in the Garden of Eden at the very beginning of time.

CHAPTER EIGHT

Despite the early night, Jayden slept comfortably late, dozing until well after eight o'clock. Nahla had made her get up and let her out around six as usual, admitting a wintry blast of cold air in exchange for the fluffy ginger body and the straight snake-like tail, carried jauntily high. The woman had scurried back to her warm bed. On waking properly, Jayden decided to use her weekend wisely, packing her favourite things into the diminishing minutes of freedom and acknowledging that Raff couldn't always be her only source of entertainment and friendship. She had no idea how long Ed planned to stick around, but then nor did Raff. The two-week gym subscription Ed had purchased was a clue.

Prizing herself out of bed, Jayden showered and dressed in clothes that would be warm, whilst comfortable enough for a brisk venture up Steep Hill. She donned comfy boots suitable for negotiating the cobbles and set off after locking up securely. She hadn't been setting the burglar alarm but recent events made her feel vulnerable and instead of occupying her hours away from home with worries about intruders, she decided to make the job a little harder for them from the start. She had begun to get complacent and the last week had been something of a wake-up call. Jayden pressed the button to arm the system and then reassuring herself that she could, in fact, remember the disarm code, left the building.

By nine-thirty, Lincoln High Street was already buzzing with shoppers. Jayden's flat was quite far north and situated where the pedestrian area narrowed. Stepping outside onto the pavement, she was pleased to see a watery sun making its hallowed appearance, relieved not to have the now familiar prickling feeling on the back of her neck of someone observing her. She congratulated herself that perhaps the sighting of her brother had only ever been in her imagination.

At the bottom end of the High Street, the pace was always fast. People shot in and out of the larger stores as though their lives depended on it, resembling contestants on a game show who had to fill their trollies as fast as they could and run to the checkout. It could be frenzied and chaotic at the wrong time of day, especially on a Saturday when women seemed to take over the town, conducting their expert shopping expeditions with military precision. Woe betide anyone who stepped between them and the bargain rail in one of the department stores.

Jayden's end of town commanded a slightly different atmosphere. Apart from a small supermarket which was the last bastion of the big chain stores, the street was filled with clothes shops and boutiques, the stuff of tourists and specialist buyers. The pace was slower and more controlled, partly due to the start of the famed incline up to the cathedral, aptly named Steep Hill. And steep it most certainly was. Most sane people required a reason to ascend it; sighing as visiting relatives insisted, or desperately needing something themselves uphill and not wanting to move their car from the expensive downtown car parks and fight in the Bailgate for a rare slot. Steep Hill was Kilimanjaro-with-cobbles to the average stroller and not for the faint hearted.

The buildings on the lower slopes were mainly three storeys with the odd four storey poked in between. Jayden was aware of other people living in the upper storeys of the buildings around her, but she never saw them. Occasionally, she would see upstairs lights glowing out into the street but anyone joining the throng of the High Street would be quickly swallowed up in its river of activity. Residents were largely invisible.

After enjoying the sunshine on her face for a moment and observing the couples and family groups strolling past arm in arm bracing themselves for the ascent, Jayden dropped into the stream of foot traffic heading north like a gentle exodus from the city. She sauntered along, in no hurry to meet the foot of the forbidding climb. Jayden loved this part of the city. The buildings nestled together like primary school children lining up for something. No two buildings were the same height, the same period or the same architecture. Each was unique, with defining features that made it special and marked it out as Victorian, Georgian, Tudor or much older. Every building style over a few thousand years was out on show, sunshine glinting off hand blown glass windows and stone carved codes in the walls and pillars, left behind by expired stonemasons as their signature. Even for the most placid, disinterested observer, it was a feast of human ingenuity and beauty for the eyes, a free demonstration of how 'different' can fit together and produce something breath-taking.

The original cobbled flags made up the centre of

the road, skilfully blended with what had once been a pavement before the area was pedestrianised. Vehicles could access the road, but exclusively to unload. The surface had been so well trodden that it was pressed smooth like glass and treacherous in the rain or ice. In extreme weather the shop keepers would salt the area outside their doors, most locals knowing to stick close to the buildings and only the tourists breaking their necks in the centre of the street. Jayden's father, Dan, had brought her here as a tiny girl. He had been visiting the sale yards and taken her along for the ride. They had climbed the hill and puffed to the top hand in hand companionably.

Dan's stories were sought after by his children, always fantastical with a hint of realism thrown in for good measure. *"Tell us another one, Daddy,"* Jayden had cried, bouncing on the balls of her feet with excitement. He had told her how as a young man in the army, he had driven a huge truck down the cobbles of Steep Hill when it was still the thoroughfare of the city, almost losing control of it on the bend at the bottom. He had described everything for her so that she could be there, a casual observer as the tired corporal had struggled to get the huge air brakes to persuade the tyres to grip the road, coming to rest precariously and embarrassingly on a kerb edge.

"There," he had pointed to a chip in the ancient concrete which he had claimed was his. "That's where the truck came to rest. Right there. Can you see?"

The kerb had been carefully changed and made to look authentic by local council workers years ago, but Jayden knew exactly where it had been, the visions of that happy, special day ingrained on her memory for all time.

Jayden strolled behind a family with four children. Two little blonde girls skipped and ran ahead, a matter of metres, the eye of the elder girl always flicking towards her parents. She was like a miniature mother duck, shepherding the other two who toddled behind whilst keeping an invisible cord attached to the smaller blonde who skipped ahead in a steady insular, oblivious rhythm. Not much older than any of them - mere months rather than years - she acted like a little sheep dog while her parents strolled behind hand in hand. Always moving, always busy, she rounded them up whilst at the same time prevented them running on. It was curious to watch, her parents seeming to have passed on their incredible responsibility to this six or seven-year-old whilst passively observing her progress.

At the corner of St Martin's Lane on the left, road works had caused the cobbles to be dug up and orange and white barriers prevented anyone falling down the large excavated hole. As though by an unseen hand signal, the little girl dropped the reins of responsibility and looked to her parents who transitioned back into authority. "Come here Charlotte," called the mother, holding her hand out to the blonde curly headed child who skipped back and held out her arm. Instantly the small boy ran back to his father on legs that didn't quite seem long enough. His gait was awkward and he almost fell a few times, his baggy pants flapping around his limbs. "We need to be careful of cars in some places," Mummy said and although no answering comment was made, the message was plainly received. The tiniest child aged around two, also curly headed with a strawberry tinge to her fine mop had already been closest to the adults and her immediate reaction was to hold out her arms to her father. He swung her up onto his hip easily and wordlessly sorted out a fracas between the eldest girl and boy, over who got to hold his remaining hand.

The tiniest girl held onto her father like a monkey, wrapping her arms around his neck and clipping her legs around his waist, her hair bouncing with each footstep. Keeping the inside of his elbow around her thigh, he still managed to reach down and hold the boy-child's hand and put the other arm around his blonde daughter. Jayden strolled behind, transfixed by their dynamic, feeling that she could easily watch them all day. It was fascinating. As soon as the danger was passed, the children escaped again like a waterfall from their father, tiny feet pouring down onto the cobbles and away they went, the older blonde child resuming her never ending mustering duties.

The Strait opened out before them, increasing in gradient and the children skipped ahead as though it was nothing. The little family turned left into a quaint, old fashioned sweetie shop and Jayden ploughed on, opening her coat against the rising heat inside. She found this part of the city beautiful. The cobbles were more ridged here and she moved up onto the smooth flags of the pavement to gain more traction under her boots. At the junction with Dane's Terrace, Steep Hill rose above her, taking Jayden north. It was one of those hills that could be powered up without stopping, reaching its crest a sweating, puffing mess, or take slowly with long laboured steps, trying to enjoy the scenery whilst sweating and puffing. It was the kind of hill best enjoyed whilst clinging onto someone else's arm and letting them do all the work.

The houses on Steep Hill were smaller and much older. Pale grey and sand coloured stone intermingled with red-bricked dwellings; some turned into shops and others with gleaming front doors into a residential home. Jayden thought it must be like living in a zoo, the constant stream of people nosing into your lounge window as they huffed past or taking photos that would appear on blogs or social media. It would feel like a massive invasion of privacy. Jayden knew that Raff struggled with it sometimes. Only the other week, a woman had shouted crossly at him for emerging from his own front door in a pair of running shorts, just as she had taken what she hoped would be a beautiful photograph of the frontage of his house. "What can you say to people like that," he had laughed to Jayden later, "when they believe that they have the right to appropriate everything their eyes see?"

Raff, as usual had been highly inappropriate, wrenching his shorts down to reveal his shapely muscular behind and then gone off for his run. He was fortunate not to have incurred a charge of indecent exposure, but he seemed to get away with most things. A tourist family somewhere on the planet would get a shock, scrolling through their digital snaps with friends and neighbours. A conversation about 'what is the world coming to?' would surely begin over the Italian's delightful buttocks.

Jayden continued upwards, enjoying the sunshine on the top of her head. It was uncharacteristically warm for January. Not warm enough to strip off to her tee shirt but enough to lose the outer layer. As the green railings began and the gradient extended its reach skyward, Jayden stopped and turned to face downhill. She slipped off her jacket and tied the arms around her waist, gazing down at the street below. The city itself was obscured by the twists and turns of the hill and the red-bricked houses which dominated her eye line. Ashamed that she was finding excuses to stop walking and catch her breath, Jayden turned and pushed on.

The street became narrower and the cobbles more uneven. Suddenly the steps up into the gathered houses seemed awkwardly placed and in the way, the front doors oppressively leaning over the pavement, making it feel crowded and far too personal. The pavement was narrow and Jayden saw a slender, red-haired woman making her way down the hill pushing a pram out in front of her. She moved rapidly, her legs shuddering with the impact of the hill as she powered down, holding onto her baby's carriage with white knuckles. Her face was fixed and her mind elsewhere as she wheeled on regardless, an accident waiting to happen to a tortoise-paced-tourist bracing the hill. Everything about her screamed *local*. It was her hill and she was using it. Jayden smiled, feeling solidarity with her, taking a backward glance into the pram as the mother juddered by. A little red-headed baby peered out at her, catching her eye and Jayden smiled before shutting off the answering connection in her heart. *A life of marriage and motherhood is not for you*, she told herself firmly.

More architecture laid itself out for admiration in the upper part of the street; Jews House and Norman House thought to date back as far as the late twelfth century. The half-timbered Tudor looking buildings gave another excuse to stand and stare or employ one's camera if the lungs were threatening to pack up, but Jayden pressed on, used to the incline from her forays up and down to Raff's house at the very top. The cobbled road was by now only just wide enough to fit one car width between the curb edges either side and could become congested with walkers at the wrong time of day, especially in the summer. Jayden enjoyed herself, walking straight up the centre, savouring the link with the millions of historical feet that had trodden them over the centuries.

The tiny street made the buildings hang over her, a patchwork of ancients touting their wares; designer chocolates, mulled wine, antiques, a veritable feast for tourists. The welcome tea rooms at the top promised a cold drink and a sit down for brave adventurers.

"Did you know," Raff once joked, "that it's possible to eat and drink your way up the hill from bottom to top?" It was a slight exaggeration, but Jayden could see his sentiment. Calling from the top of the rise was the beautiful black and white Tudor building, turned into luxury holiday apartments.

Feeling the cobbles under the soles of her boots, Jayden turned right at the top and strolled towards the imposing gothic cathedral, feeling as though she had all the time in the world. It was the nicest sensation.

After paying her entry fee at the cathedral doors, Jayden peered up at a small stone imp tucked away in the 'v' joint of the vaulted ceiling.

"Do you want me to show you where he is?" an elderly volunteer asked. She had sparkling blue eyes and a kind face, her back misshapen and bent with age.

"Oh, I know where he'll be, thanks," Jayden smiled down at her, turning her head to fix her eyes on the sullen, stone figure above their heads. The lady patted Jayden's forearm and shuffled away to help someone else.

The imp looked so tiny from down below that he could easily be mistaken for just another decorative carving, left by a skilled and inspirational craftsman. The presence of the 'Lincoln Imp' was portrayed on postcards, souvenirs, jewellery and crockery, all helpfully stocked in the cathedral shop and selected stores down in the city. He was the town mascot, the 'thing' that united locals and even graced the name of the city's football team, 'The Imps.' The presence of the creature was massive, given personality and character by the use of his small grimacing face to give a rural town a visible, marketable edge.

The rigidified demon returned Jayden's curious gaze through his passive blank stone eyes; his rugby ball shaped head dipped towards the ground and his little horns on obvious show. The up-lights gave the imp a sinister air, darkening his eye sockets in strong shadows and casting a black line across his chest. Tiny hands with stumpy fingers rested on a leg that was bent across in front of his body, one cloven foot resting on the knee of the other as he slouched casually. The stone was sandy, yellowed with age and atmospheric pollutants which floated around unseen, slowly degrading everything. Yet the cathedral had stood through centuries and survived the continual molestation of more pressing threats.

Jayden kept her face upturned, mulling through the folklore that accounted for the creature's existence. His life story bedecked the brochures and pamphlets at the entrance to the cathedral and in a hundred places elsewhere in the city. Only he knew the truth. Was he the devilish outpouring of a stonemason's chisel or the legendary demon of the local stories? Would Satan, the father of lies, really take the trouble to send a tiny demon to Lincoln Cathedral simply to cause trouble? Legend stared in the face of logic and cried, 'Yes!' So there he sat, frozen rigidly in position for more than six hundred years.

"I can't see it," came the voices, suddenly close to Jayden as she looked at the source of all the curiosity. The cathedral contained many beautiful features including a library designed by Sir Christopher Wren and an original of the four remaining copies of the Magna Carta. Instead, tourists chose to look upwards with cricks in their necks to see a tiny imp in the rafters that was not much bigger than a coin from the stone flagged floor below. Jayden found herself crowded by the tourists, who had been frog-marched to the spot by their eager guide. They milled around impatiently, catching sight of their quarry one by one and marvelling at detail they could only see in the brochures clutched in their expectant hands.

Jayden sighed and moved away, seating herself quietly in one of the chairs behind them. She loved to 'people-watch,' allowing herself to believe that she was involved with their lives purely from the looking, spared the chaos and potential problems which real interaction brought with it. The little family from Steep Hill was among the throng, the children whispering loudly that they couldn't see the imp. "It's not there," the boy complained.

Their father lifted them one at a time, brightly coloured sneakers dangling from stick-thin ragdoll legs, bouncing harmlessly against his thighs. The

Trojan effort was not in the lifting of four little individuals, but in his belief that the extra six feet nearer the ceiling it put them, would help them to spot the miniature trouble maker. Jayden smiled as each child squealed with glee and pointed, claiming to have spotted the naughty impish face. The Lincoln Imp continued to grin widely, his sharp stone teeth barely visible from the floor as he kept the secret of a multitude of beaming tourists. To many he was simply invisible and they had to pretend.

Jayden glanced around her, sensing the calm and drawing it into herself. The cavernousness of the building tended itself to silent prayer and meditation. Visitors naturally hushed their voices reverently and moved around in quiet groups. It wasn't just respect that caused them to do this but the tumultuous echo which copied each and every loud noise, repeating it over and over about the lofty heights and embarrassing the maker for moments at a time.

Shifting her jacket over her knees, Jayden spotted a man sat at the other end of her row of chairs. He bowed forward, his forearms resting on his thighs and his hands clasped firmly in front of him. A chunky knitted grey pullover graced his strong looking body; a large collar folded up to protect him against the sunless interior of the stone building. His hair was dark and tousled and his fringe hung in front of an olive-skinned face, hidden from her by the angle at which he sat. Jayden crushed her rising, impolite interest and sat back against her chair, closing her eyes against distractions.

The peace of the familiar building washed over her, the breath of its former inhabitants wafting her in waves of unique air, trapped inside the ancient structure. The smell of aged stone was more comforting than unpleasant. Behind closed eyelids, Jayden pushed through her worries and concerns, handing them over to her maker with relief. She didn't pick through them one at a time, lacking the energy to revisit the myriad niggling thoughts. It was like trying to contain spiders in a matchbox. Even the tiniest chink would encourage first a spidery leg of worry to emerge, quickly followed by the whole damn pile, entertaining pre-empted scenarios through which to wander aimlessly and get largely nowhere. Jayden mentally took the box and plonked it squarely at the feet of Jesus, knowing that he had the ability to sort through and order it all. The trick was just to leave it all there though and resist the urge to take parts back.

Temporarily satisfied with the relief that prayerfulness inevitably induced, Jayden gathered her jacket towards her breast and stood up. Another knot of tourists were grouped to her left, blocking her exit as they stared up into the rafters seeking the tiny creature responsible for all the fuss. It forced Jayden to move to the other end of the chairs, realising too late that the dark haired man still occupied the end seat. She stood deliberating for a moment. No matter, it wouldn't be a difficult manoeuvre to shift the centre chair and move it back. Unfortunately on closer inspection, it was found to be joined on either side by a selection of clips that held it firmly in place. *Climb over then.*

As Jayden stood reflecting on the possibility of a clown-like exercise, whereby she attempted to clamber over the back of the plastic chair and ended up on her face amidst a clatter of plastic and metal, the man at the end of the row stood up. Jayden's hair, hanging loose around her shoulders and spine in a riot of bouncing curls, swished uncontrollably around her face as she jumped at his sudden movement. Emerald green eyes focussed quickly in his direction.

Raff's older brother looked back at her, clear blue eyes in his peaceful face. A protrusion of light stubble betrayed a habitual Saturday neglect, but it sat well on his dark looks. The tentative smile was sincere as he opened his right hand and offered Jayden safe passage from the seating area. Thanking him she sidled past, trying not to brush against his body in the small gap and wishing that he would step out into the aisle. He didn't. Presuming that Ed intended to sit and resume his quiet time, Jayden nodded to him and began to move away, surprised by the rough sensation of a masculine hand grasping hers.

Jayden reacted as though she had been stung, withdrawing her hand instantly and gripping it in her other one, almost in an enforced count of her fingers. Her jacket fluttered to the floor and Ed watched her curiously before bending to retrieve it. "Sorry," he said shaking his head in annoyance at himself. "I didn't want to speak too loudly in here, but I wondered if you knew exactly where the Lincoln Imp was. Everyone is looking up there, but I haven't been able to spot it yet."

Feeling foolish, Jayden accepted her jacket from his outstretched hand, careful not to touch his long, dark fingers. Her smile failed to make the distance to her eyes and she nodded as pleasantly as she could muster. It would be a task of a few minutes and then she could escape, back into the peace and quiet of her deliberately lazy weekend.

Ed stood close to Jayden as she pointed upwards

at the roof. "There," she jabbed her finger at the grumpy, face overhead. The stone pillars arced gracefully downwards from pivotal points on the white plastered ceiling. Despite her outstretched arm indicating the presence of the tiny stone vandal smirking from his vantage point, Ed seemed unable to distinguish him from the other shapes gathered about his tiny body. "Look, he's lit up," Jayden pointed for the fourth time as Ed peered fruitlessly upwards. "I don't know why you can't see him. He's got his mouth open and little teeth on show."

Ed looked exasperated and huffed crossly. "Maybe I need glasses," he commented wryly and Jayden couldn't help but smile. "What's his story anyway?"

Jayden dropped into the role of tourist guide, reciting a tale as familiar as her own assumed name. "Allegedly it was the imp's attack on the Angel Choir sometime in the fourteenth century which angered an angel. The beautiful winged guardian was pelted with pieces of stone, aimed more at annoying than injuring and in return, the imp was turned to stone for his antics."

Ed nodded appreciatively at his guide's enthusiasm and momentarily carried away, Jayden glanced around her, making sure that nobody was in sight before hauling Ed backwards towards the seats. She clambered awkwardly onto one of them and then leaned over Ed's high shoulder so that she could see from his angle. It was exactly what Dan McGowan had done with his precious Lily so many years before. Her father's generous nature and good-will washed over her, in a rare comfortable dousing. "Not there!" she exclaimed. "You're looking at the wrong pillar. He's up there, look."

She positioned her fingers on either side of his jaw and tilted his head backwards but at the same time to the left, until she felt his body abruptly still at the sight of the Lincoln Imp. "I thought he was bigger somehow," Ed breathed in wonder. "Little troublemaker."

Jayden laughed and climbed down from the chair, aware of an embarrassed flush creeping up her neck to her face. She had made a protective mental decision not ever to have physical contact with any eligible male and yet here she was, laying across Ed's shoulders like a girlfriend. *Or a wife. Shame* compounded her difficulties, crippling her with the accusation and squawked rebuke. Nine years of relatively comfortable spinsterhood was being threatened by an oblivious stranger.

Ed's dark lashes flicked as he kept his eyes fixed on the demon. Threads of grey peppered his sideburns and fringe, making him appear weathered and illustrious. Jayden hovered awkwardly as she waited for dismissal, her mission complete. "Time for coffee," Ed surprised her, clapping his hands together once in satisfaction. "My treat. I don't understand why I couldn't see him; he's really obvious."

"Perhaps you're a closet local," Jayden smiled kindly. "The guide I came round with the first time said that once you felt as though Lincoln was your home, you were blessed with the ability to just walk in and look up and there he'd be, waiting for you. The imp, not the guide," she giggled nervously. "Every time I came here for the first year I had to ask someone to point him out but then one day, I walked up the hill and just knew exactly where he would be. I found him the first time and I've never struggled since. But before that, it was like he hid from me." The pretty girl looked wistfully up towards the organ pipes in the distance.

"What was different - about that day?" Ed asked softly and Jayden's brow knitted in confusion at the question. She took a step back from him as though finding him potentially dangerous.

"Enjoy your coffee," she said with a false smile and walked back towards the enormous front doors. Ed felt the waves of *Fear* and *Confusion* emanate from the young woman, causing him to shiver. She intrigued and perplexed him like something forbidden that must not be touched. The trouble was that it made her even more enticing.

Gazing up to the spot that Jayden had directed his face, Ed was astounded to see a coiled stone shape facing back at him, a carved bauble much like the others on the pillar. His head whipped from side to side like a frustrated tennis spectator, but the imp had obscured himself from view once again. Ed sighed and ran his hand over tired eyes. It would have been almost funny if it didn't suddenly feel so damned important.

CHAPTER NINE

On Monday morning, the Reverend McLean resembled a box of extremely excited birds, flitting and fluttering with nervous anticipation. His new curate was due to arrive, as he repeatedly told anyone who would listen as he floated around near the front doors of the church. "He's very experienced," McLean announced to Sal on reception, as he made a foray into the counselling centre. "Apparently he's well thought of up at the diocesan office. He's not the one that I was meant to get, but this one is much better."

Sal rolled her eyes at the monologue that spoke about a working man as though he was an exchanged toy. Reverend McLean shook hands unnecessarily with a congregation member who had been trying desperately to hide in the seating area. The poor man blanched at the cleric's sudden interest in him. Cam was treating him for the origins of a deep-seated marijuana dependency and the middle aged man knew that if the vicar even got a hint of his particular trouble he would hound him out of the church.

Cam bouncing enthusiastically out of his office provided the release for his client from the grips of the vicar, who seriously looked as though he was going to ask why he was there. The man ran into the safety of Cam's office as though the hounds of hell were after him, leaving the vicar thwarted in his quest for knowledge. The old man stood in the centre of reception for a moment, twisting his hands in annoyance before remembering his new curate. That caused his face to light up beatifically and put the spring back into his step as he went back to stand by the front doors.

"This is the Reverend Edward Smith," McLean announced proudly an hour later, displaying his new curate with aplomb. Cam stepped forward to shake the new toy's outstretched hand, but Jayden gaped somewhat like a trout. Raff's brother raised an eyebrow and appealed with his eyes for her to just go along with the ruse.

"Hi," she said lamely, thinking, *no it's not - it's Eduardo Abbadeli*, but allowing him to take the fingers of her right hand in his strong ones anyway. Jayden detested weak handshakes, taught how to make her mark on the world by her father with a firm, masculine grip. Her hand in Ed's resembled a lettuce that had been in the sun too long, the rest of her body consumed with surprise and dismay at an apparent deception.

Ed's strong jaw was visible through the skin of his cheek as his teeth ground against each other. His manner was calm and assured, but the glances he darted towards his brother's friend betrayed fear that she would out him. She didn't. Jayden detached herself from the little charade, relieved that she was employed and salaried by the diocesan offices and in essence, had no need to become embroiled in the machinations of St Jude's.

McLean was thrilled with the novelty of his new gadget and marched Ed off to meet Brian and explore his new surroundings. As he led him through the doors towards the main church, Cam laughed as the reverend's voice echoed back to them, "Only I'm allowed up onto the balcony above the nave. It's the rules."

He sounded like a small child in primary school, forbidding anyone to touch his new bicycle and the naked obsequiousness in his speech was raw and jangling. With a smirk at Jayden, Cam retreated back into his office, leaving Sal and the counsellor gazing after the clerics. "Hot!" Sal commented with a lascivious smile. Jayden knitted her brow and declined to answer, going back into her room and closing the door.

Curiosity taunted her, pushing her to text Raff and tout for answers as to Ed's odd behaviour, but she shoved the thoughts away. If he wanted to change his name, that was his business, just as it had been her choice to do the same. Raff had texted Jayden on Saturday afternoon, asking if she was all right after her sudden exit from the gym. She had reassured him that she was fine, but wondered if it was the truth.

Ed had asked her a poignant question at the cathedral when she had been showing him the imp. He had asked her what was different about the day on which the troublemaker's location had become irrevocably clear. It had been just another buried thing in the armoury of Lily McGowan's existence. It had been because of Rita.

"Forgiveness is part of healing," the lecturer had been saying, grabbing the attention of the packed undergraduate class. Her orange hair had moved in an unseen breeze, but even the humour of that had failed to dull her words. They were words that Jayden had not wanted to hear, not right then. *"It's a documented fact that rape victims able to forgive their attackers put*

themselves voluntarily into a better place for recovery. Oh, it's not an instant fix by any means. It doesn't happen just by saying the words. But it is a process of the mind, an act of letting go which with it, brings considerable release."

Many of the students had shifted uncomfortably in their rows. Rita also taught a Christian counselling paper as well as this psychology lecture and they waited for the bible bashing which was sure to come. It didn't. She put up a PowerPoint slide depicting facts and figures and left it at that.

Jayden had the proverbial 'aha' moment, as though a nugget of rocket science had just dropped into her soul. Her next tutorial with Rita had brought the first, in a series of honest admissions from Jayden. "Forgiveness is a two-way street," the girl had argued. "I won't go to see him, to tell him that he's forgiven so how will he ever know? And doesn't he have to apologise also, for..." it was difficult to say the word out loud. She tended to think of it as the 'attack' rather than give the incident more power by using the actual term.

"Who are we talking about?" Rita had asked. Jayden had looked at her feeling instantly indignant that in all their sessions, the woman had failed to absorb what she had been told. Perhaps she wasn't interested. Maybe she saw so many students in this degree that they all blended in together, their problems mingling and overlapping.

But Rita had continually emphasised the need for clear, concise notes, precisely so that such forgetfulness could not happen. Jayden knew that she wouldn't have made that mistake. She sat looking blankly at her tutor. Rita sought to clarify things for her most promising student. "Are we talking about the man who raped you, Jayden? Or are we talking about the one who betrayed you?"

Jayden had gulped. While the thought of Wes thrusting around on top of her filled her with horror, disgust and revulsion, the image of Nick's boyish, pleading face caused a knife-like pain just under her ribs. Whilst she had been prepared to try and forgive Wes one day, his abuse of her body being completely in keeping with his twisted character, she couldn't even contemplate forgiving Nick. He was her older brother. She had looked up to and adored him; acne and attitude included. He had sold her to his dealer for a single hit.

The Victim Support counsellors had touched on the word 'betrayal' also, but Jayden had recoiled from naming the thing, afraid that if she did she would then have to deal with it. This particular day had seemed different in a nondescript way. Rita had asked her if she could forgive her brother and it was as if Jayden had known right then that she couldn't, but that it had suddenly become a possibility somewhere in the future. One day she would most definitely have to, even just for her own sanity. It was as though her world opened up a little more, forcing a crack in her splendid isolation. She didn't have to face it now, but it was there, hanging over her like a threat.

Jayden had made the steep climb up the hill from her lecture theatre near the Brayford Pool. Recognising her as a regular visitor and local, the door guard at the cathedral refused her money and waved her through the turnstile. Jayden had known that afternoon that the imp would be waiting for her, high up in the rafters. Sure enough, he was there, grimacing from his perch triumphantly. He embodied the wicked things in life and Jayden had raised one finger towards his cocky little face, warning him, "I know your game!" She was more than aware of the demons who flanked her daily. Knowing each of them by name, she recognised their trademarks and resisted them as best she could. Simply knowing their names and their torturous intent was never going to be enough though and Jayden had devoted the remaining seven years to trying to banish them from her thought processes and decision making. Some days it was as though she had succeeded, but on the bad days they hung around the sides of her face like irritating sarcophagidae flesh eating flies, taunting her and buzzing noisily in her ears.

The honeymoon period between the Reverend McLean and Ed Smith lasted a day. To have credited the peace with a full twenty-four hours would be stretching the truth because they were arguing before the close of business on Ed's first day. The vicar's temper went from excitable to vicious within a matter of hours as the new curate made sensible suggestions about offerings, congregation members, finances and buildings, all with the very best of intentions. The staid vicar preferred to call it 'interfering' and got increasingly upset as the day wore on. "You don't know what you're talking about!" he bellowed finally, at the dark, handsome man in front of him.

Ed was punished with the most minor of roles when he arrived for work on his second day. There would definitely be no preaching for him! He was trusted only with the role of organising the little group of elderly women who voluntarily arranged the flowers to decorate the front of the church. At the start of each year, they sat down with the vicar and with much grumbling and gnashing of teeth on his part; they formulated their themes and worked out their roster. Ed infuriated McLean, taking the women into the church coffee shop and treating them to lattes out of his own pocket. He had them entranced within a very short period of time and the roster was worked out, typed up on his laptop there and then and printed off in the church office within a fifth of the time that it usually took. "Bye ladies," Ed said, his deep blue eyes oozing sincerity as the octogenarians fawned over his proffered handshake. Ed was acquiring fans and it was a dangerous game around McLean.

McLean's game was to have everyone like him. He had to be the most needed person in the building which is partly why he pontificated so ridiculously, drawing out the decision making in order to look important. He was famous for his 'let me sleep on it' line, which would never engender a result, not even if the man went into a helpful coma for the remainder of his career.

The handsome curate was garnering way too much kudos for the vicar's liking, frowning deeply as he watched the women leaving. He couldn't be completely sure, but it looked as though Mrs Tischel had been about to kiss the curate's hand. John McLean was shocked. How dare Edward Smith come in and make friends so quickly! It had taken *him* years.

To the delight of the sycophantic Brian, Ed's jobs became worse. He was given the delightful task of dragging last autumn's leaves out of the lower guttering and the wide drain lines which ran around the side of the old building. The black cassock which McLean insisted on his curates wearing at all times was discarded for such jobs and replaced by a boiler suit which Ed must have found in the groundsman's shed. Jayden felt unreservedly sorry for him.

When McLean rushed off for some ultra-important deacon's meeting late on the Wednesday, Jayden took a cup of tea out to Ed, who was sluicing out the bins belonging to the coffee shop. "He can't make you do things like this, surely," she complained in hushed tones. "It's not right. Brian's asleep in the pews again and you're out here, freezing your..."

"It's fine," Ed chided her gently, taking the steaming mug gratefully in hands that were almost blue. "Jesus preached servant-hood. Perhaps it'll be good for me."

"Well, if McLean tries to make you wash his feet, I'm calling the bishop myself!" Jayden exclaimed. Ed put his head back and laughed, a deep, jolly sound which resonated off the stone brickwork melodiously.

"There's no need," he said, burning his lips on the hot drink and jolting slightly. "It will all be ok."

He looked so helpless, standing there in his blue boiler suit, his hands shaking from contact with the hose pipe's freezing water. His lips had gone a dreadful shade of purple that showed just how arctic it was outside. Completely out of character and done more from a feminine nurturing instinct than anything else, Jayden reached up and laid her warm palm against Ed's cold cheek. His skin felt rough and tight against the elements and Jayden pitied him. "This is wicked," she said, injustice leaking from her voice. "I'm going to do something about it."

Embarrassed at the physical contact, Jayden withdrew her hand quickly and turned on her heel. Ed called after her, surprising her greatly with his response, "Jayd, don't. Please. I'm begging you. *Don't.*"

His eyes implored her to stay out of his troubles. He didn't look downtrodden or bullied. Nor did he look as though he would bow to pressure, in the same way as the weaker Brian had done, caving in upon his florid self horribly. If anything, Ed looked as though he had all the time in the world and if Jayden was not completely mistaken, was enjoying himself more than a little.

Confused, she returned to the building, cringing at the drop in temperature to below zero, which surely made hosing out dustbins the most miserable of tasks. Ed continued for the rest of that week and the start of the next, in buoyant good humour and resounding popularity despite the dreadfully menial tasks entrusted to him. He changed light bulbs, electrocuted himself mending a fuse on the mains box when McLean 'accidentally' flicked the 'on' switch while the wire was still in Ed's hand and also increased his friendship base amongst the staff in the coffee shop and the enchanted congregation. It was as if the more McLean abused the man, the more he gave off an ethereal glow which only served to make him additionally attractive.

Jayden complained to Raff when he popped in one evening after work. "Leave it babe," he insisted. "My big brother knows exactly what he's doing."

Jayden doubted that very much somehow and toyed with the idea of ringing the bishop herself. With the exit of Bishop Pargetter, there was some hope that the new one might not be part of the Old-Boys'-Network. But Sal had told her that he wasn't in the post yet and it stood to reason that the acting post-holder would not be keen to open up this particular can of worms and then run off into the sunset. It sat badly with Jayden's sense of injustice and she determined to intervene in the very near future.

CHAPTER TEN

Jayden was usually strict about her timekeeping. It was part of showing herself respect by valuing her own time. Clients weren't permitted to approach either her or Cam in their private time, encroaching on their lives and families like a hungry ocean eroding a victimised shoreline.

Once a client built up a relationship with someone who had the tools to improve how they felt about themselves, their marriage or their psyche, they would often adopt that person in a relationship founded on need. It was dangerous and something that Jayden and Cam were constantly aware of. An hour appointment meant an hour appointment, no more, no less, although Jayden was much better at self-imposed deadlines that the generous-hearted Cam.

Cam had been the subject of an unfortunate infatuation by a middle-aged spinster, who had shared her deepest darkest secrets with him a few years ago and had certain expectations in return. Her possession of him had been ghoulish and frightening as a woman crippled by loneliness had fantasised and dreamed of ownership of the handsome, capable man. It had been crippling for him and for his gentle wife, who had endured weeks of hostility every time she set foot through the doors of the church. The vicar had been incensed when Cam and his family found another church to patronise on a Sunday and he doggedly refused to understand the poor man's dilemma. It was a common problem and while Cam had received the full support of his supervisor and Jayden, he had angered the pig-headed vicar for all the wrong reasons. For McLean, it was merely about bums on pews and coins in the cloth offering bags. "He's disloyal!" the vicar had raged.

The foolish old cleric should have stepped in and had words with the client but was consumed by his own fear of confrontation and failed the counsellor due to his personal inadequacies. It had been a shocking episode, distressing in many ways, but the elderly bishop, angrily approached by Cam's supervisor, huffed and puffed and achieved nothing but bluster. Perhaps he had fully intended to reprimand his old friend as he called him up to his sumptuous residence near the cathedral. But after a shared whiskey and an expensive cigar, he couldn't quite remember why the man had called. The reverend headed home, having gotten away with yet another failure in his duty but bizarrely held poor Campion responsible and hadn't spoken directly to him since.

Jayden had finally begun getting somewhere with a teenage client who had taken forty minutes to open up to her. Throwing him out at dead on five o'clock seemed ludicrous and so she had broken her own rules and continued to the next available moment, guiltily aware that his long-suffering mother was waiting outside. One of the written rules of counselling in this environment involved issues surrounding deliberate personal harm. All clients signed a contract at the start of treatment, forcing them to understand that any threat of harm to themselves or others would immediately invalidate any confidentiality agreement. The sorry young man in front of Jayden admitted to cutting himself with a razor blade, regularly and in moments of extreme stress as a release. "I never mean to," he mumbled. "But it just seems to help." With the blood-letting, often came a welcome relief from pressure and a regaining of control. But it was a decidedly slippery slope down which anyone could potentially lose their footing and fall, unexpectedly or otherwise.

The man-boy was sixteen years old. He was clad in a scruffy grey puffer jacket and a dirty black tee shirt, sporting the name of a famous rock band peeked out at the world. His jeans barely held themselves up around his backside and a pair of loud silky yellow boxer shorts yelled out at the back. His hair was lank and greasy and his face speckled with an unhealthy smattering of large, painful spots. He would be nice looking one day. But not today.

He had only come to counselling because his parents, having reached the end of their rope had threatened him with Social Services. Tough love. Shape up or ship out. Whilst other parents may posture and criticise the harassed adults, it was not Jayden's place to judge them. Desperation spoke many languages. The boy was trying to shape up, but underneath the razor cuts and the attitude was a debilitating ball of pain, hovering just beneath the surface of the young heart. "I hate my dad," he said, chewing unattractively on a hang nail.

Jayden could almost see the spirit of *Death* hanging around him like a curtain, telling the boy in him that he was worthless, a disappointment who would be better off dead.

The root of it - the dysfunctional relationship with

his father - would undoubtedly come as something of a shock to the strong patriarch who had done his best to fulfil his role as hunter-gatherer, taken his son to soccer games and tried his hardest to link in with the boy. As was often the case, despite best efforts, the pair misfired and failed to connect. This was the result; one man oblivious and the other damaged and left open to the whispered lies of those familial demons who filled his time and thoughts.

The young man was gently dismissed with homework and some strategies for coping with the raging bull inside him, which would rise unbidden and force him to resort to tried and tested methods for dispelling its influence under pressure. Campion was floating around and Jayden sat with him in her office for a while, getting his input on the course of action with the young man. His injuries had been old and well worn, smacking of an addiction that was possibly as old as him, venting his anger like the valve on a pressure cooker. With the poising of the blade came anticipation, fear and a mingling of hope, followed by the cut and certain but temporary relief. But there was always the risk of suicide and Jayden would be failing in her duty if she didn't seek the confidence of a colleague. It was what she had been trained to do. Campion gave her sound counsel and then their chat turned to the attitude of the formidable Reverend McLean. "I'm never certain whether the man is completely incompetent or an extremely adept manipulator," Cam commented, unwinding his long legs from their seated position.

Jayden humphed. "Well, the jury remains in deliberation on both counts. But he can't be allowed to carry on treating his new curate like that. It's awful."

With an affectionate pat on her shoulder, Cam left for the day and Jayden stayed to write up her notes. It was too hard to remember once time had elapsed and there was a tendency for one client to meld into another. It was after six when Jayden finally closed and locked her office door, drawing the buttons of her coat together over her smart suit. Outside in the foyer as her heeled boots clicked across the thin carpet, the timbre of raised voices caught her attention. Jayden halted for a moment, fighting conflicting urges. Curiosity told her to investigate, to involve herself in the reason for the argument while the wise, knowledgeable side of her screamed at her to leave, to get out and disassociate herself from the fracas. The tape in Jayden's head which she struggled to control, yelled at her that *trouble is dangerous*, turning her feet for her and pointing them towards the glass exit.

On stumbling legs, Jayden overrode her survival instincts and walked slowly towards the door which connected the administration corridor to the counselling suite, recognising Ed's placating voice interspersed with the vicar's angry raised one. Through the glass, she spied the two men squaring up to each other in a narrow corridor, banners depicting Jesus in various parables and poses ironically dangling over their heads from bamboo canes.

The Reverend McLean was apoplectic with fury, his face puce and pulsing, the veins standing out on his neck as though something fairly major was going to burst. Ed, by comparison, looked calm and in control. While the vicar postured and lurched unsteadily on his feet, the younger man stood casually leaning against the wall with his hands insolently in his pockets. "How dare you!" the vicar was practically screaming. "Who the hell do you think you are?"

Ed's face was impassive and his expression bland as Jayden observed through the glass, but the elderly cleric was hysterical. His black shirt strained at the buttons and his white collar hung down on one side. His large rounded tummy protruded over his tight belt as he alternately lurched and feinted. He flapped at his overheated face with pudgy hands and had evidently lost control of himself. Ed's black shirt and slacks were impeccable and his dog collar was perfectly placed. The only 'tell' that he was anxious was the way that he ran his right hand through his smooth dark hair and his blue eyes flashed dangerously as the vicar's voice reached an irritating screech.

Jayden's defence mechanism won through and turning, she quickly and silently left the building, making sure that the badly fitting door made no sound as it buried its lock in the door jamb. She wondered what had happened that had set the vicar raging so badly. His temper was a latent beast, usually content to lie dormant and be vented in overeating or bullying as the man serially avoided those things that made him feel inadequate. He would always choose the underhanded route over the confrontational, such as forcing Ed to wash out the bins rather than talking to him about what was making him angry.

Occasionally, however, he had been known to explode periodically, usually in the face of some disappointing behaviour on the part of Brian. Mysteriously too afraid of his subordinate to actually reprimand him, the vicar would roar around the church, picking over minor issues and honing in on those who were unlikely to answer back or defend themselves against his unreasonableness.

Ed had looked nonchalant and clearly had things well under control, giving the older man time for his clockwork mechanism to run aground. Jayden hurried up the high street quickly, remaining vigilant and watching for anyone showing too much interest in her passing. Again she felt the prickling feeling as though someone was watching her. Crossing Silver Street she panicked and hailed a passing taxi, finding herself at Raff's front door in a highly emotional state.

CHAPTER ELEVEN

Raff was glum and upon letting Jayden into the house, took her hand and led her upstairs to the kitchen where he opened a very expensive bottle of Cabernet Sauvignon. He sat in a chair next to her at the table, the wooden struts digging into their backs and put his arm possessively around her, not giving her time to remove her coat even.

The scent of aftershave and male deodorant moved comfortably under Jayden's nose as her senses relaxed and she permitted the feeling of safety to enfold her. Raff had showered after his very physical day and his dark hair was still damp. Jayden snuggled into his armpit with the frightened tears drying in salt trails on her cheeks, controlling her staggered inhale and exhale motion to persuade her body to seek its equilibrium again.

Raff sipped his wine one-handed, periodically kissing Jayden's damp temple, his arm firmly around her shoulders. Jayden was thankful that he asked no questions. The kitchen was still with the gentleness of a shared companionship; the Aga clicking gently in the corner as it heated water for the radiators and taps. It felt like heaven. Jayden sat up slightly, wiping her nose inelegantly across the back of her hand, but Raff kept his arm firmly around her shoulders, heavy like a dead weight. He kissed her temple again but then his face moved down alongside hers and to Jayden's surprise he kissed her cheek, before placing his wine glass carefully on the table and with a smouldering look, kissed her gently on the lips. She pulled back slightly in confusion. Raff was a physical person, requiring the affirmation of touch as badly as his lungs required air. He did often kiss her but this was different. His eyes held a curious glint and as he reached up with his hand and pulled her head in close to his, an unfamiliar electricity arced between them and he kissed her again, longer and with more intent.

"No!" Confusion raced through Jayden like a tornado, tearing at her insides and displacing everything she thought she had known. She stood up quickly, shoving her chair back across the floor with the backs of her knees and causing it to smash loudly into the cupboard behind. Raff was left, sitting half turned in his chair, his hand still raised in the air at the point where Jayden's face had been, that curious look still on his face. Jayden's heart pounded, sending too much blood around her body to swish noisily past her ear drums and her face flushed red like a traffic light. She put her fingers up to her lips as though not quite believing what had just happened and then she decided to leave.

Reading her face perceptively, Raff jumped to his feet and seized Jayden's arms, pulling them around his waist and drawing her into him. The possessiveness had gone from his body and she was unafraid. Worse was the feeling which remained, the sensations that she had denied herself ever having, content to dwell in spinster-ship for the rest of her life. Her body betrayed her, reminding her brain that it had never signed any such agreement and that despite her traumatic and devastating first sexual encounter, it was possibly willing to venture there again.

"I'm sorry," Raff whispered. "You just looked so vulnerable and I wanted to take care of you. I'm sorry."

Jayden pulled away from him with an enormous, unladylike sniff and looked up into his face, concern tinged with betrayal. "But you're gay!"

Raff made to kiss her on the forehead again and then thought better of it. He let his arms drop to his sides and went to sit back down in his chair. Jayden remained standing as he cupped his wine glass in the palm of his hand, the glittering, crystal stem dangling between his ring and baby fingers. "Peter and I are over." Regret and misery dripped from his words. "My heart wasn't in it and he was totally obsessive. After the other night, we had a massive argument and I called time on it. He was absolutely livid. I'm glad Ed ran off after you. I would have been humiliated if he'd heard the things Peter said to me." Raff bit his lip and turned to face Jayden. "I've been thinking. We could be really good together, you and me. I mean..." he took another sip of wine and got into his stride, adding weight behind his flawed argument with each spoken thought. "If we got married, there wouldn't have to be anything sexual, but we would both seem normal somehow in the world's eyes. I know you're not interested in guys, or girls, but it could work out really well. Maybe we could even have a family...by IVF," he added as the horror crossed Jayden's face. He stood up and crossed the room, more confident now that she hadn't overtly rejected his proposal - or him as a person. He put both hands on either side of her face and stared deeply into her perplexed green eyes. "You are my best friend in the whole world Jay. You would want for nothing, I promise. We could make it work. Please think about it?"

His voice was pleading and slightly higher than usual. It was ludicrous and yet the thought took root in Jayden's rational mind, the promise of company, of no more lonely evenings, no more aimless, empty weekends, the opportunity of normalcy. Her scrambling brain kept her silent, focusing on the black and white floor tiles, neatly patterned and uniform. Every day, common or garden, *normal*.

As the word 'normal' reverberated in her mind, it felt like a ping-pong ball popping off the insides of her skull and Raff's words took a different slant suddenly. He wasn't 'normal,' of course he wasn't. He was gay! But he was lumping her in with him, tainting her with his hidden brush and saying that she was in there with him, in the socially unacceptable club of abnormal people. Surely that couldn't be right. Hidden prejudice doused Jayden with indignation and anger so that Raff's words, which had been intended to soothe and unite, ended up cutting and tearing at her friendship with him. "You're homosexual! Why do you deny who you are?" Jayden's voice was raised and incredulous.

"Me denying who I am? That's rich! What about you? You live in constant denial of who *you* are!"

Jayden was stunned, looking angrily at Raff and wondering at first what he meant. Then as the dawning realisation came, pressing and thrusting into her consciousness she felt sick. Years of intensive counselling, being counselled and then turning her dreadful experience into compassion and an outworking of genuine kindness had been a complete waste of a life. Raff was right. She was in denial. She had denied herself and the beautiful flower name that her wonderful father had chosen for her. She had denied her family and especially her poor widowed mother and worst of all, she had denied her destiny. Her *real* self ached to be loved, to be cossetted and appreciated, desired and cherished. It cried out to her from deep in her soul, buried and forgotten, the childish girl inside who had clacked around in her aunt's wedding shoes, holding up the too-long meringue dress to prevent her from falling over the hem. The small, slender Lily had pranced and twirled, the zipper hanging agape at the back and her brother laughing at her and pretending to be her groom, upstairs in the loft of the little Welsh house.

Jayden's body revolted against her suppression of its true nature and it felt as though her whole being turned on her ruthlessly, exacting its revenge for almost nine years of imprisonment behind the bricks of her emotional fortress. The deep red wine pressed itself back up into her gullet and she clapped her hand over her mouth as it threatened. She was utterly undone.

Raff's blue eyes were wide in his handsome face as he powerlessly watched his best friend become unpicked at the seams. *Guilt* overwhelmed him and even as he reached out with pathetic, flailing hands for her; Jayden was gone. She fell down the bottom three steps of the richly carpeted staircase, the smooth bottoms of her stockings adding a further betrayal to the list. She ran, leaving the front door open like a gaping, surprised mouth as she bolted out into the street, her boots still in her hand.

The slick cobbles were slippery and unforgiving to unshod feet and Jayden slipped again, ending up on her bottom in the middle of the wide courtyard. To her left, the tall cathedral peered spikily down on her, lights glinting out of the lower windows and peeking around the doorframe. It beckoned to her gently to come, to find solace and comfort inside and relief from the demon laughing on her shoulder, but the broken woman shied away from its invitation, already irreparable even to God.

Realising that Raff may still come after her, Jayden shoved her feet into her boots and set off running down the steep pass at a dangerous pace. It was breakneck at the best of times, but her increased forward motion, encouraged by gravity's intention to set her back at city level made the going treacherous. Jayden concentrated on the painful bruise which signalled that internal bleeding had begun around her tailbone, blackening and creating perfect hues where she had fallen so hard. Her left elbow ached in her rough sleeve and she cupped it in her right hand. Her work clothes were wet and stained with street muck at the back, but she hurried on regardless, her handbag abandoned on Raff's kitchen table but her spare front door key kept safely hidden on the leather thread around her neck. It nestled between her breasts and promised that its sanctuary would enfold her, allowing her to heal behind the portcullis of her front door and re-establish the image of the capable, independent-counsellor-of-other-people's-problems, in peace.

Jayden clopped hazardously on her boot heels, finding herself in the same spot where she had ended up on her knees a few nights ago. Again the smooth rail bar came to her rescue, slamming against her hip bone and preventing her uncontrolled descent for just a second as she cruised like an out of control race car. She hit the soft wall at a furious rate, crashing into it with no chance to brace herself against the impact. One minute it was just air in front of her and the next, a solid black cushioned shape which let out an '*ooof*' of pain as she ploughed into it.

Strong hands steadied her by her wrists, pushing her gently upright from the unfortunate body that she had smashed into. Jayden uttered a hurried apology to the man and detached herself, trying to step carefully around him despite the forward downhill pull that encouraged her feet to dance with it again. But he held onto one of her wrists and as her brain recognised his voice, her heart plummeted back into her boots and the sickness returned. "Jayd? Are you ok?"

Ed's face peered into hers, a carbon copy of Raff's but without the complications of his sexuality marring the image. Jayden's eyes were wide and her pupils dilated and black, obscuring her green irises almost completely. Her nose was running and tear stains streaked her high coloured cheeks. The clip that had kept her hair under control all day, now lay smashed on the cobbles outside Raff's house and dark curls bounced and danced on her shoulders, around her face and down her back. But worse was the desolation which oozed out of her as the curate kept hold of her delicately boned wrist.

"Row with Raff?" he asked, an edge of something indiscernible in his tone and when Jayden looked away from him, unable to explain, he kept hold of her wrist and turned his body in towards her swiftly. He pulled at the rest of her arm and used his other hand to tuck her elbow under his companionably. "I'll walk you home."

Jayden aligned her body with his, feeling the smart

of her painful elbow underneath his fingers. It was becoming almost unbearable. But concentrating on the pain outside was preferable to dealing with the ugly, spewing mass on the inside and so she allowed the bone to rub and grind and ignored the seething mass within her soul. Once outside her front door, she struggled to extract the bulky mortise key from inside her clothing, fighting one handed to haul the leather string from under the collar of her blouse. Ed helped her, his fingers strong and gentle, pushing her hand away as she wrestled to release the warm metal from the folds of her bra and to lift it sensuously from her skin.

Jayden's heart clamoured so hard that her brain denied the physicality of anything else around them, forcing her just this once, to remain in the moment instead of bolting to some safe place in her head. It was as though her entire being had overrun her volitional mind and determined to break out once and for all. Everything that had ever been good about her rioted violently, shocking the demoniacs from their perch. *Suppression, Isolation* and *Despair* let go for a while, waiting for a moment to return quietly once the fuss was over. *Depression* hung around in the wings waiting for his chance too.

Ed battled valiantly to get the cord over her head and snagged tendrils of tangled hair in his gallantry. Finally, the key was in his hand and slipped easily into the well-oiled lock. He stood back politely to allow Jayden to pass and that was when she saw the delicate bouquet resting on the bottom step. Ed must have stepped over them to get to the door. A bunch of white lilies poked closed heads from a florist's wrapper, bobbing their creamy bonnets in the breeze from the street. They couldn't have been there long. Otherwise someone would have stolen them for sure.

Jayden stared down at them in terror, knowing instinctively what they meant, the high colour from the emotion and the walk leaving her face instantly. Ed looked at her curiously and bent to retrieve them for her, wondering if his errant brother had sent them. Jayden pushed him away from them, gasping as her elbow connected with the rock hard surface of the man's chest and she kicked the delicate blooms out into the centre of the walkway. Ed stood poleaxed as Jayden moved painfully up the front steps to deactivate the burglar alarm at the keypad in the downstairs hallway, watching as she sat on the bottom step to remove her boots and rub at the painful soles of her feet with her right hand. Glancing over his shoulder at the broken bouquet littering the Lincoln street, Ed ventured slowly up the steps and over the threshold like a watchful bird which cautiously approaches the bread-laden hand, ever aware of the danger.

Jayden swiped her hand across her eyes and then used the cuff of her coat to wipe her nose while Ed made his decision and entered the hallway more boldly, shutting the front door, locking it and kicking off his smart, black work shoes. He held the threaded key out to her, observing her in an eerie glow from a nightlight which was plugged into a socket at floor level, noting how she winced with pain as she reached up to take it from him.

Wordlessly Ed helped the beautiful, dishevelled woman up from the step and pushed her in front of him. Lamps were already on upstairs casting a serene, romantic pall over the open space. It smelled of flowers from an air freshener on top of a kitchen cupboard, vanilla and jasmine, but not a hint of lily. In the light, he could see the grey, wet stain at the back of her long coat where she had fallen and Jayden dropped it from her shoulders and left it where it lay, rumpled and empty on the carpet. She gripped at her left elbow which looked swollen already through her blouse and her face was a mask of pain and other emotions, too complex for Ed to read.

Inappropriate, inappropriate, inappropriate, the sensible mantra screamed inside his clerical head as he helped her off with her blouse, concentrating on the sickening bruise that surrounded her funny bone and had already begun to stretch down her arm. He found a packet of frozen peas in the room behind the kitchen, tied at the top with a little metal tag. He brought them back to her and fixed them around her elbow with a tea towel, wincing at the hiss of pain that escaped her lips at the icy contact, or was it at the touch of his fingers perhaps?

Ed found the bottle of wine which she had drunk from days ago when they had shared dinner together, untouched since. The cupboards bore no other alcohol, but the pantry yielded a partially used bottle of cooking sherry. He poured a decent glug into a glass for Jayden and took it to her, amused by the face she pulled as she downed it like a child being given nasty cough medicine. "It might just take the edge off the pain."

Ed laid the glass on the dining table and reached out towards her. She looked so vulnerable and childlike, standing in the huge room in her pink bra and work skirt, her discarded blouse and coat at her feet. The grotesque scar just under her ribs contrasted starkly with the silk of her flesh, angry and livid in its six inch awfulness. Ed wanted to cover her up, to protect her, surprised at the strength of feeling in his heart for her. In the absence of anything close to hand, he put his arms around her and pulled her into his body, his black clerical shirt feeling too rough to be permitted to nestle against her creamy soft skin.

It was inevitable that the proximity of two full blooded heterosexuals with a mutual attraction would lead to first one kiss and then another. Ed melted under the helpless naivety of Jayden's tearful kisses, feeling the wetness of her cheeks as she responded to him with hesitation and then desire. Raff's earlier kiss and subsequent accusation had released a beast within Jayden; a bound and restrained lover that did not want to be put back into its box and it both frightened and exhilarated her. In truth, she had thought it killed stone dead by the rapist's hateful ministrations in exchange for her brother's last fix and spent the intervening years peppering soil over its burial ground, unaware that it was not dead but dormant and very much alive.

Jayden's suppressed feelings for Ed blossomed as dynamic and hopeful as a schoolgirl crush and the Lily part of her bloomed like her discarded bouquet on the street, currently being rescued by a delighted pedestrian.

CHAPTER TWELVE

Ed had started it and so it was right that he should end it. Reluctantly and long after he had known that he should, he pulled away from Jayden's welcoming lips and with a sigh of regret, turned away from her to collect himself. Jayden faltered helplessly, realisation dawning as she stood vulnerable and naked in her bra and skirt by the dining table. The ugly spectre of *Abandonment* laughed at her from the corner of the room, opening its filthy maw and leaking her destruction for the second time in her life. "This is wrong on so many counts," Ed struggled to meet her clear, sparkling eyes.

Jayden's face, which only moments ago had been tender, yielding and responsive, closed with a snap in front of him, locking him out with shades of rejection and hatred. It seared his desire with a jagged, defender's blade and left him feeling breathless and empty even though she had said nothing.

Ed strode over to the stairwell feeling a mixture of clown and torturer. He shut the front door gently after him, worrying about whether Jayden would come to lock it, but hearing the snap of the lock and the drawing of bolts as she must have followed him down the long staircase.

Jayden ran back upstairs, jolting her elbow with each step taken, forcing her up the next staircase to vomit spectacularly in the toilet of her ensuite. The sickness stayed with her for most of the night, releasing her only to lie on the bathroom floor in a painful ball for a few hours. The pain was physical, manifested in dry retching and stomach tearing heaves but it was also emotional. The awakened seventeen year old Lily did not like the severe, guarded woman she had become and was desperately trying to break free from Jayden's enforced imprisonment of her. But out with her leaked a whole world of trouble, formerly dealt with and locked safely away. With Lily came the memory of Wes' dirty hands on her young body, his ruthless enjoyment of her against her will and the muffled screams which bounced off his sweaty collar bone. And the face of her daddy as he had burst in to save her, his final look of compassion and dismay for his daughter only, as Wes' blade slid into the generous, loving man who had named her, mentored her and died for her.

At five in the morning when the retching finally stopped and she felt safe enough to leave the bathroom, Jayden sat in her lounge with a cream woollen throw wrapped around her bare shoulders. A notepad rested on the sofa cushion next to her and her shaking right hand gripped a blue biro. The grinding of the bones in her left arm had long since told her that it was broken and the blue and purple hues had leaked through onto both sides of the joint. She knew that she needed to get it fixed, but she had to do this first.

Treating herself as she would any other client seeking to recover from a trauma such as rape and the cruel betrayal of a cherished sibling, she made notes, asked rational questions and dealt with the tears. None of this was new. Jayden had been over this ground enough to know it intimately, but she pushed herself anyway, looking for that elusive key which would unlock the final door to her release. The last time she had done this had been recently with Rita in attendance, congratulating herself that she was a finished work of art, a success story in the making, the perfect example of recovery. She had slammed the trunk lid even harder on Lily's memory, bisecting herself deliberately because deep down; Jayden had known that it wasn't over, it wasn't finished and she wasn't recovered. On top of Lily's grave, deep within her soul Jayden had piled the lies, versing them until she was sure that they had become a part of her original plan, *I do not want a relationship, I do not need a partner, I am better off alone.* The only success was that she had begun to believe her own lies which fed the excitement of the demons who rode her mercilessly into splendid isolation.

It was perhaps ironic that the kiss of a gay friend; himself confused about his sexuality and life path, had caused the trunk lock to pop. But it was Ed, his deep, aroused need for her which had burst open the lid, shifted the soil and left this awful gaping void. Jayden knew that she had two choices; she either stuffed it all back inside and returned to the comfortable, safe, empty life that she had forged for herself or she looked deeper into the chasm and finally faced what was there.

Jayden believed in God. She knew that he was there with her now and that he had been with her on that awful day. She understood none of it and reasoning and pleading the 'why' question had got her nowhere, but she trusted him now to take her out of the despairing pit of desolation because he always had before. The demons of her making could sit on her shoulder and knead at her head with their knotty fists, but they could not possess her. Because of God she was free from that threat, but boy, they could make her life a living hell if she let them continue to ride her shoulders like a fairground attraction.

With a deep, ragged breath, she drew the five decreasing circles, one inside the other like Russian dolls and began right back in the beginning. It was a bit like making a jigsaw, fitting together the pre-cut shapes blindly without knowing what the final scene was meant to be. Jayden forged her way through them all, her physical circle, her emotional circle, her volitional circle which contained her will, her drive and the force of her being. She halted for a while there, trying to work out how her life goals may have skewed themselves, reassigning other, more realistic ones and putting a line through those she no longer wished to pursue. She scrubbed out the sentence *to stay safe* yet again, deciding once and for all to leave that to a higher power altogether, having failed miserably on her own account. It was where she usually stopped, knowing that she would fail and be back chanting the wrong tape again soon but for once she pressed on further, trespassing deeper into the locked cellar of her heart.

Her rational circle gave her the most trouble, a myriad of conflicting mental tapes and sentences playing on repeat in her brain, worthless and contradictory under examination. She crossed them out and replaced them with only one in their place; *I am loved*, adding underneath it, a list which comprised of her mother's name, her aunt's and her God's. Her spiritual circle came last, trisected by the need for every human being to feel significance, self-worth and security. *And there she found the key.*

She had probably always stopped short because she had inwardly known exactly where it would be, nestling under the ashes of her childhood, waiting to be collected.

In her mind's eye, she reached out for the glittering gold of its smooth surface even as her fingers twitched in the real world above. It was comfortingly old and worn, drawing respect for the great and cumbersome lock which it could bend to its will. It would never have been effective held there along with the detritus of broken dreams, disappointment and dented pride. It was not possible to create any of those three fundamental human requirements for oneself. Significance, self-worth and security were God-given and Jayden had been on a hiding to nothing right from the start. She had helped hundreds of people find their own keys over five years of counselling, celebrating with each one with generosity and excitement as they unlocked their dungeons and went on to live without her. She had always dropped them off at the door, unwilling to share the last part of their journey because she couldn't go where she had never been herself. *Wholeness.*

CHAPTER THIRTEEN

It was not easy to shower one-handed or get dressed again either, but somehow Jayden managed it. Her handbag at Raff's house contained her mobile phone and she was forced to use the old one with hardly any credit to call a taxi.

With damp hair shoved messily into a ponytail and no makeup on her face, Jayden went to sit at the Lincoln County Hospital Accident and Emergency Department for a few hours. It was early enough not to be too crowded and she was eventually seen, triaged, x-rayed and encased in plaster. The result was a small fracture of the bone at the end of her forearm, apparently called the olecranon. The fracture appeared to have stayed in line and Jayden was relieved that it would not require surgery. She calmly accepted the pain killers offered to her and dialled another taxi from the hospital lobby.

The time in the waiting room had been productive. Undisturbed by the other patients around her, the room had dulled to a low hum of activity and Jayden had done some more much-needed processing of herself and her feelings. She recognised that part of her reluctance to fully deal with her inner circle had been because unforgiveness stained the walls of it like a submerged cave continually attacked by the ocean. She simply hadn't wanted to see. Unsure at that moment quite what she could do about its presence, Jayden took it one step at a time and felt content that at least now, she had been reminded yet again that it was there and its hold on her psyche would be short lived at best. She was finally going to do something about it.

The taxi driver dropped her off on Saltergate, kindly getting out of the vehicle to help her out, with her cast and sling hindering progress greatly. "Thank you," Jayden was grateful and walked down to her flat, stopping in the centre of the thronging mass of bustling city-goers in the mid-morning rush to observe the little knot of male figures at her front door hammering on the wood.

I am not afraid, the tape played robustly in her head and she hastened over to the men, her face a look of worried expectance.

They turned as one to look at her, two uniformed officers and two in smart suits. The policemen in uniform looked like schoolboys, their adult clothes, a mark of authority clanging awkwardly with their acne and the innocence in their faces. But the plain clothed cops were world weary, although polite. One was in his late fifties, married judging by the gold band on his ring finger, but the other was Jayden's age, blonde and good looking. Unusual brown eyes smiled playfully out of a clear skinned face, eclipsing the other officers in his model's gaze. He was hot and he knew it.

The frown on Jayden's face and her non-plussed look revealed instantly that she had no idea why they were there. "Is it my mother?" she asked the younger detective, walking up close to him even as she fidgeted with the irritating sling.

He shook his head, *no*. "Jayden Mitchell?" he asked her, equally softly and as she looked up at his taller frame, she was close enough to see the light flecks in his hazel eyes. She nodded.

The older detective flashed a warrant card, depicting a younger and much fitter man whilst indicating his head towards the door and Jayden retrieved the key on its leather thread from the right front pocket of her jeans. Unfortunately, the action caused her wallet to fall from her fleece pocket, spewing coins from the taxi fare all over the pavement. It was an old one that she had dug out from the bottom of a drawer, her proper one being stuck up in her handbag in Raff's kitchen, another casualty of her unpremeditated flight.

Passers-by stopped to watch the two uniformed officers grovel around on the wet concrete for money, while a burly detective opened a door that most of them had never noticed before. The motley crew proceeded into the flat and up the stairs, juggling around each other in the narrow hallway while Jayden re-locked the front door behind them. Eventually, she sent the policemen ahead of her to her living room while she removed her shoes and rued the fact that none of them gave her the same courtesy. Perhaps bare feet or holey socks were not conducive to successful interrogation.

The uniformed officers milled around the room looking at things without touching, while the detectives stood and watched her. Jayden felt hot and wanted to get her fleece off, made difficult by the fact that the nurse had helpfully put the sling on over the top of her clothing. In the end, she walked to the kitchen and flicked the already full kettle on. Nobody said anything and irritation splashed Jayden's pale cheeks with spots of pink. If it wasn't her mother then she really had no other concerns. It wouldn't have taken four cops to tell her that her brother was out of prison, which she already knew and they would have called her Lily and not Jayden, if that were their purpose.

The reason that her wallet had fallen so easily from her pocket became obvious as Jayden reached in and pulled out a bottle of tiny white tablets and a large cream box of yet more drugs. She tried to undo the bottle, desperate for a hit of the codeine inside which promised to still the throbbing in her elbow and resorted to using her teeth.

The blonde detective came over and held out his hand for it, reading the label before easily dislodging the smooth lid. "Is that recent?" he asked her, nodding towards the sling. Jayden's smile held pain and exhaustion, a wretched, sleepless night followed by a morning of discomfort.

"I was walking back from a friend's house last night in the rain. I slipped over on the cobbles uphill. I kept ice on it last night, but it was such agony this morning that I got a taxi up to the hospital to get it checked out. It's broken." She sighed ruefully, "Now I'm too hot."

Jayden tugged at the sling and then gave up, surprised when the policeman ventured around the counter and lifted the knot up and over her head. The nurse had somehow left her cast out of the fleece, but then got it trapped under the sling at the neck. Jayden gratefully let the sling fall into the policeman's hands and shrugged her fleece off, noticing with horror that her coat and blouse were still on the floor by the table, where Ed had left them the night before. A flush of embarrassment lit her face and she looked away, lest the astute detective read anything in her expression.

"Would it be all right with you, Miss, if we checked the property?" the older detective piped up and Jayden looked at him, suddenly alarmed. The uniformed officers seemed rapidly attentive like guard dogs waiting for the order to spring on her. It occurred to her that they had already been surreptitiously looking for something.

"What's going on?" she asked, widening her pretty eyes at the blonde officer whose name she had already forgotten. He was pleasing to look at and she indulged this new side of her nature, aware that she may be surprised by the things that crawled from the trunk in her soul over the next while. She felt flirty and it was a completely new phenomenon for her.

The other cops disappeared upstairs to the bedroom level in their street shoes. Jayden controlled a fleeting exasperation at their lack of consideration. Didn't they care that his was her *home?*

"Please can you tell me your movements yesterday?" the policeman asked with a smile. He had perfectly straight white teeth with enough character not to look horsey. He offered Jayden the sling back and when she shook her head in refusal, laid it on the counter and drew out an official looking notebook from his inside pocket and flipped it open in one smooth, practiced movement.

Jayden exhaled slowly. He stood very close to her and yesterday she would have moved back, her sole intention being to get away from the masculine threat of him. Today she stood her ground, aware of the new game unravelling inside her, a fearlessness born of the realisation that the worst of life had already befallen her. There was little this man could do to her, to humiliate or harm her more than had already been done. It gave her a new and addictive courage which seemed to come from the soles of her feet, arcing over her body like a gossamer dome. *God is responsible for my safety.*

"Sorry?" the cop said, looking curiously down at her and Jayden realised that she must have murmured the phrase out loud. She smiled and looked embarrassed.

"I think it would be more polite if you helped me make myself a drink to take these tablets with and then explained to me, exactly what's happened. And then I will tell you everything I possibly can."

CHAPTER FOURTEEN

She hadn't been expecting that!

"You were seen locking the office up after six last night and it was noted that it was unusually late for you."

"I've told you three times now why I was late going home. I didn't see anything. This is all too much to take in."

Jayden wasn't quite sure why she was lying to the handsome detective, but she suspected that he was aware of it. It was probably why he kept asking the same questions over and over again, even though the tea he had made her was long drained from the cup and the pills were beginning to cloud her brain and dull the ache in her arm. All she wanted to do was go for a lie down. "Who told you they saw me?" she asked suddenly, knowing that it couldn't have been either of the clerics because they hadn't seen her.

"I'm not at liberty to say, Miss," the detective continued, brushing her enquiry aside. "Why did you not get a taxi to Mr..." he consulted his pocketbook, "Abbadeli's house from work? Why did you walk all the way up here first?"

"I just wanted some company. It gets lonely at home by myself sometimes and Raff is my friend. I walked home and then decided I wanted to be with other people. I knew he wouldn't mind. It was a split decision."

The uniformed policemen had left together;

straight-faced and empty handed. Jayden wondered what her bedroom looked like, judging by the 'looking' that they had done downstairs. They hadn't quite wrecked the place, but they had moved things. Jayden's neat-freak tendencies fought her. The older detective had gone outside onto the roof garden upstairs and Jayden could hear his muffled voice through the open door, distorting as it carried down the spiral staircase to the living room. Her bedroom would be freezing when she finally made it up there; which would hopefully be very soon.

She eventually heard a click as the sliding door was closed and locked and his heavy footsteps trod down the stairs still in his shoes. He closed a mobile phone with a snap and slipped it into his pocket and then seized a dining chair and slumped heavily into it. Jayden's heart sank as her desperate need for rest was pushed further and further back in time. "The taxi driver has confirmed that he picked up a young woman on Silver Street last night around six thirty in the evening and took her to the top of Steep Hill, where he watched you knock on the door of a house there and enter." Jayden sighed with relief, but the officer hadn't finished. "He also stated that you were rather distressed and he asked you if you were all right."

Both of the policemen looked hard at her. Jayden faltered. Her arm felt as though it had been trapped in some kind of heavy machinery that was still crushing and pulsating over the bone and her sleep deprived brain had ceased to function normally. She closed her eyes and prayed for divine help, knowing instinctively that God wouldn't help a liar. At no point had she mentioned seeing Ed rowing with McLean. She knew that she should, but the words wouldn't seem to come up to the surface and meet her tongue.

A heavy knocking sounded on the door downstairs and Jayden stayed seated, expecting it to be the policemen returning with a search warrant. Surely that was the next natural progression of this mess. When she opened her eyes, the young blonde policeman was smiling at her but Jayden was far too tired to care. The other man clumped heavily down the stairs and opened the door, speaking roughly to whoever was on the front steps.

Ed appeared at the top of the stairs, having thoughtfully discarded his motorbike boots at the bottom. He undid his tight leather jacket as he came into the room, his black clerical shirt and white collar looking incongruous under the biker attire. He kept the leather pants on over his work trousers.

"You can't leave that bike there," the older cop jibed as he puffed back up the stairs, clearly getting more than his usual workout. Ed ignored him, barrelling straight over to Jayden.

"Oh crap!" he said, spotting the cast lying on her thigh under the table. "We should have gone straight to the hospital; I'm so sorry. I didn't think it was broken."

Oblivious to the two other men in the room, Ed squatted down next to Jayden's chair, noticing how dreadful she looked. Dark rings circled her eyes making her look as though she had been thumped in the nose and her body language was of someone defeated. "You look shattered," he stated the obvious. "I don't suppose you got much sleep. Sorry, I left you. I should have looked at it better. We were worried sick when you didn't come in this morning, especially after...they told you I guess?" Ed jerked his head in the general direction of the policeman sitting across from her. Jayden nodded sadly.

"I can't believe he's dead. The Reverend McLean. Murdered. It just doesn't make sense," she said to him quietly.

Ed ran his hands through his hair leaving his fringe sticking up like a cockerel's plume. He stood up and assumed his full clerical authority, addressing both men with a voice that dared them to challenge him. "Miss Mitchell is plainly unwell. If you have no further business here, perhaps you won't mind returning at another time?"

The policemen glanced across at each other, but neither of them moved. Ed hadn't finished.

"Did you find a murder weapon here? No, I guess not. Do you seriously think that someone Jayden's size could have tipped a large man like Reverend McLean up and over the balcony rail after clubbing him across the back of the head? I guess that's a 'no' as well. So if you don't mind, either you leave or I will call a lawyer and force you to state your case formally."

That did it and with a grunt, both men left the flat, stepping crossly down the stairs to the street. Jayden made to get up as the front door closed, but Ed went back down to turn the key in the lock. By the time Ed had run nimbly up the first flight of steps in his socks, Jayden was already upstairs and headed towards her bedroom. All she could think about was a clear path in front of her, leading to the sanctuary of her bed.

Ed found her standing helplessly gazing down at the neatly pulled lilac bedspread, which revealed the corner of a plush matching duvet. He looked at her curiously, noticing out of the corner of his eye that she seemed to be fiddling with something at waist height. As he turned her slowly to face him, he saw that she was struggling to undo the button on her jeans with one hand. He gently moved her fingers away as her head drooped, released the ornate rivet and pulled the zipper down. His full lips parted slightly, but Jayden pushed his hands away and moved towards the ensuite, where she removed her jeans with stubborn difficulty.

Leaving her tee shirt on, Jayden abandoned her jeans on the floor of the ensuite and stumbled out of the room and across to the bed. It felt so far away from her that she allowed the growing delusions to take hold momentarily and cheat her of the anticipated peace. With every step forwards it was as though the bed moved tantalisingly away. Ed's guiding palm in the small of her back was both welcome and torturous, but she made it to the bed, scrambling in carelessly and letting out a hiss of pain as she banged the cast.

Her head safely on the squashy pillow, Jayden exhaled as safety washed over her. A gnawing emptiness in her stomach disturbed her but the retching was long since done with and she was determined not to go back there to the place of desolation. Ed squatted down next to the bed, his long fingers caressing stray strands of hair back from Jayden's forehead. His voice was soft, like a lover's as he spoke gently to her, "I was worried when you didn't show up for work today. Nobody had heard from you so we kind of assumed the worst. Especially with..." He didn't finish his sentence.

"What happened?" Jayden asked, but her speech

was lazy as the codeine and the drug they had given her at the hospital mixed and mingled in her tired, empty body, colluding and conspiring to form a haze of confusion.

"Don't worry about it now, Jayd," he replied, his rough, stubbled cheek resting gently against her temple as he continued to stroke her hair.

A vision clarified itself urgently to Jayden as she plunged into the nothingness. The Reverend McLean was purple with rage, posturing and dancing on uncontrollable feet as he shouted at Ed, '*How dare you?*' But before Jayden could lay a proper hold of the realisation that came with it, she was gone, plunging down into welcome oblivion where there was only floating peace and absolutely no pain.

CHAPTER FIFTEEN

When Jayden woke two hours later, she felt infinitely better. The deep sleep had made up in quality what a day's worth of catching up on her wretched night might have achieved. She was immensely thirsty and needed the toilet, but her broken bone had dulled to a bearable throb which may well feel the benefit of some more painkillers.

She stumbled out of bed and into the ensuite, not bothering to close the door behind her in the empty flat. She flushed the toilet, washed her good hand and most of her bad hand with difficulty and attempted to clean her teeth. It was easier to splodge out a ball of toothpaste onto the side of the sink with her right hand and then try and scoop it up with her brush, than do it traditionally when she didn't want to disturb her elbow overly much. Somehow she managed, feeling heaps better now that her mouth tasted less furry.

The sound of someone coming up the stairs caused her eyes to widen in fear and Jayden stopped dead, half way between the ensuite and her wardrobe. If she had an intruder there was nothing she would be able to do about it, not with a broken arm. The colour drained from her face like water furiously leaving a bath and she was frozen in place as she realised that Ed must have left without locking her street door.

But it was Ed's handsome face which came slowly into the room from the landing. He had stayed. "I didn't want to scare you," he said, as though soothing a terrified deer, "but I'm sorry. I can see that I already have."

Jayden could only nod fractionally, paralysed despite the fact that she was standing in front of the curate in a tee shirt and knickers. He walked over to her and put his arm around her, leading her to sit on the bed. He sat down close next to her and Jayden felt suddenly embarrassed about her lack of makeup and the bird's nest of hair on her head.

Ed had worn his forty-two years well. His dark skin had shrugged off its early morning shave and black bristles peeked through as the day waned. Crow's feet decorated the corners of his intense blue eyes, displaying a man that in other circumstances perhaps smiled and laughed a lot. His work at St Jude's had not been easy and it was probably now public knowledge that he had clashed with the Reverend McLean on numerous issues. It had been a flashpoint, the older man's flagrant disregard of budgets, misuse of church funds for silly fripperies instead of major concerns and other too numerous issues to dwell on. Surely the police would be heading his way very soon, once the gossips began relaying their poison to the pleasant, blonde cop.

Jayden realised a deeper emotion in play, seeing suddenly that she was jealous of the fortunate woman who got to stand next to this man in his duties, growing heated when she thought of their sinful kiss the previous night. She detached herself from his embrace and hardened her heart to the blossoming affection. He was right. Any relationship between them would be wrong on so many counts. "Will you take over, now that the vicar's gone?" she asked, ashamed of the wistfulness in her voice. *Disappointment* surged through her as Ed shook his head.

"No. This role was just temporary. I have somewhere else to be eventually but I'll stick around until a replacement arrives."

"I think you were right last night," the words stuck in Jayden's throat like glass and she hesitated before pushing on. "This relationship would be very wrong, not least because of your vows, but lots of other reasons."

"What other reasons?" he asked, surprising Jayden with the question - as if being a married curate indulging in an affair wouldn't be reason enough.

"I'm not sure that I would be quite ready, even if there was nothing in the way. I had a...bad experience a few years ago and swore off men for life. It's only recently that I actually feel like I'm healing enough to even contemplate a relationship one day."

Ed heaved a sigh of sadness that astounded Jayden as they sat close together on the lilac duvet. He ran his hand across his face and she heard the bristles rubbing against his fingers. "I'm so sorry. I'm not quite sure how to counter that. I'll keep my prying questions for another time. I should go Jayd. Sal's rung me four times. The cops are pulling the church apart. You look way too good sitting there in your knickers and I am a cleric after all."

He smiled and the origin of the crow's feet was displayed in all its glory. He kissed the side of her cheek gently and then the mattress shifted underneath her as his weight left it. His black shirt was untucked and he had taken off the dog collar and undone the top two buttons. Looking longingly at Jayden, Ed gave a small wave and left the bedroom. She listened to him moving around downstairs, collecting his gear together and leaving. At the sound of the front door closing, she went down and locked it, laying on the sofa and watching daytime TV rubbish for the remainder of the day. Ed had left her a drink of tea with two codeine pain killers neatly popped out beside it.

Despite her previous misgivings, Jayden took the pills, drank the drink and slept the slumber of the just.

CHAPTER SIXTEEN

Jayden arrived at work the next day wearing an interesting assortment of easily installed clothing. Elasticated black pants were overlaid with the only tee shirt that would go over the awkwardly bent cast and a classy denim jacket clung to her shoulders with one arm flapping. It was neither professional looking nor practical in the January freeze. Flat black zip up boots complimented the ensemble, specifically chosen for their ease to put on and protection against slipping in the ice and breaking something else. Jayden had considered a taxi but felt vaguely suspicious of the driver who had betrayed her to the policemen. It was wholly irrational as the man had only been truthful, but it had brought a heap of trouble to her hidden front door that she had not needed.

She need not have worried about her dress as the counselling rooms were closed and sealed with police tape insisting that the general public should 'Keep Out' and she had major difficulties gaining admission herself. Two telephone calls later and production of her driving licence, hastily and fortunately retrieved from its home in the front of her underwear drawer, ensured her access but the church was dead and silent. Jayden's office door was unlocked, but the filing cabinet containing the privileged secrets of her clients was still secure. Only she and the director of the diocesan headquarters had a key to that.

Jayden was just sifting through some papers on her

desk when a sharp rap at the door heralded the arrival of the blonde police officer with the brown eyes. He smiled pleasantly at her and ventured into the room. He wore a grey suit today and his hair was carefully spiked on end. Jayden smiled back and waved her good arm expansively. "Did you find anything else to suggest that I am the Reverend's killer?" she asked, teasing him. "Oh, apart from my distress on the night in question and subsequent broken arm."

The policeman laughed and sat down in her client's chair, resting his black, leather-clad binder on his thigh. "Don't take it personally, Miss Mitchell. Everyone is a suspect in cases like these."

Jayden sat herself down on her comfy chair and faced him across the desk. "Cases like these? Do you find yourself investigating a lot of murdered vicars, Officer?"

The policeman smiled, giving her a lopsided smirk. He engaged with a bit of harmless flirting in the hope that she might release the information that he suspected she was hiding. Flicking at an imaginary fleck of dust on his trouser leg, he looked up at her from underneath his lashes, observing her collectedness and beauty despite the pain in her face presumably from the break on her arm.

"So what has *actually* happened?" Jayden asked him directly, "And why is it being considered a murder? Why don't you think the vicar just fell off the balcony? He was always up there wandering around. He often squawked down at the curates and choir boys; it was his preferred method of catching them up to no good."

"Have *you* ever been up there?" the policeman countered. Jayden shook her head.

"No. I don't like heights and to be honest, Cam and I rarely have cause to go into the church during the week anymore. We work through here and when I go to church on a Sunday, I just come in the main doors like everyone else. I've never worked out where the stairs are for that balcony."

"There's a door in the vestry."

Jayden looked surprised. "Wow, like a priest hole? How exciting. I suppose that's why the balcony was so well hidden. I wouldn't have known it was there until I looked up one Sunday and Reverend McLean was looking over the side above the altar. There's so much decoration in the stone that it would be impossible to distinguish it from all the other shapes up there."

Jayden leaned against the back of her chair and tried to relax under the gaze of the perceptive brown eyes. Policemen made her feel uneasy ever since the attack and subsequent proceedings. It had taken her years to get over the feelings of dirtiness and humiliation, the hideously personal questions and the hidden feeling that somehow it had all been her own fault. Jayden crossed another chasm as she calmly contemplated the policeman opposite her and successfully banished *Guilt* and *Resentment* at what he represented. She smiled, seeing the effect it had on his bearing and confidence. "What's your name?"

He sat straighter in his seat. "Detective Sergeant Chris Lambert," he replied. There was something about him that was quite endearing.

"I realise you probably told me yesterday. But I was in too much pain to take it all in."

Lambert nodded in acknowledgement of that fact. "Is it any better now?"

Jayden looked down at the cast nestled inside the cream sling. It pinched slightly and began to itch. "Well, I will never understand how children seem able to bounce back and go to school the day after a broken bone is cast," she said pensively. "I feel like crap today. I'm going to look at them skipping along with a new found respect." Her brow knitted slightly as she remembered something. "What were you looking for in my flat? It took ages to put it all right. I was a bit slow; I didn't even ask you if you had a warrant."

"No warrant," Lambert answered, "but the full co-operation of the home owner."

Jayden shook her head and raised one eyebrow, acceding to the cunning that allowed them access to her home. It was a dirty trick, especially seeing as she hadn't been firing on all cylinders at the time. Watching her thought process, Lambert was quick to add, "We could have got one if we needed though. It would have just taken a bit longer."

"But what were you looking for?" she repeated.

The policeman shifted position in his seat. "The murder weapon."

Jayden was confused.

"You said he was pushed off the balcony."

"Actually you said that," he replied, displaying the subtle interrogation method which had shot his boyish looks up the ranks of the Lincolnshire Constabulary at a rapid speed. Jayden's face clouded as she thought about where she had heard it. *Ed.* Ed had said it as he had arrived at her flat yesterday. He had said that she wasn't strong enough to tip the vicar over the balcony. Her brain seemed to whirr and clack as the cogs turned inside and the policeman watched her casually. *Ed would be strong enough.*

"What are you *not* telling me, Miss Mitchell?"

Jayden cringed and shelved her reservations. Why was she so reluctant to tell him about the row she saw Ed having with the vicar on the night he died? Did she really think that Ed had gotten so furious that he had killed a man? He hadn't looked out of control, standing nonchalantly with his hands in his pockets as the older man had raved, but people could do the most out of character things. If her own experiences hadn't told her that, then her counselling had.

With a fleeting moment of dismay, Jayden considered her brother. Obviously he was out of prison and hanging around the city. What if he had approached the vicar for information about her and McLean had refused? She dismissed that thought immediately. Nick already knew where she lived as he had watched her walk home oblivious and laid lilies on her doorstep. That quite apart from the fact that the gullible vicar would have thought nothing about giving her address to anyone who asked for it, in complete contradiction of all data-protection legislation.

Jayden ran the scenarios through her head and still the policeman calmly observed. Leaning forward slightly, he surprised her by asking for the key to the filing cabinet containing her counselling notes. Jayden sat back and shook her head. "You will definitely have to get a warrant to do that," she said. "Unless of course, the diocese orders me to hand it over, which unfortunately I would still be unable to do. When I left my friend's house the other night, I neglected to leave my handbag at his, so I'll need that back first as the key is inside." Jayden shuddered at the thought of going up to Raff's house and asking for it. "Get the warrant and I'll allow you access, but these clients trust me. Often it's the only thing we have in common and I won't break that trust for anything."

Detective Chris Lambert entered into the game, seeing that she was distracted and preparing to go along with whatever Jayden had planned. He kept her talking for another hour, making scant notes on his pad that appeared to relate to nothing but the small talk they were engaged in. She told him nothing in essence, but he kept pressing, knowing that there was more to this woman than met the eye. She was composed and delectable, but he could almost smell the spirit of *Fear* that hung around her office waiting to swoop. It unsettled him and made the hunter in him frantic to discover what it was that she was hiding.

The counsellor was as difficult to interview as her Japanese colleague. The detective wondered if they had taken a special course in how to avoid direct questions at university, perhaps in a room labelled '101.' Cam had been evasive when Lambert had visited him earlier, simply stating that he had met with Jayden in her office and left around twenty minutes to six. His wife had confirmed that he arrived home at six having stopped at the supermarket for ice-cream as she had texted and asked him to. The receipt bore out his story with its digitally stamped time.

Lambert stared hard at the woman in front of him, knowing instinctively that she hadn't killed the vicar but sensing that she knew something significant. Jayden feinted and dodged with skill and evaded his probing, whilst wondering why she was bothering. Perhaps Ed had told them everything anyway. "Have you spoken to everyone else?" Jayden asked him casually.

"Like who, in particular?"

Jayden felt irritated at the gridlock, knowing that she had just given herself away. Lambert smiled his pin-up beam, a peculiar glint in his eyes. "I wondered if anyone else had seen something that might be helpful," she blagged, hoping to put him off the scent.

"Who would have still been here?" her combatant pushed. Jayden's heart sank and she tried to keep the inner dismay from reaching her face. She sighed in feigned irritation.

"I have no idea, Officer Lambert. That's why I was asking you."

The detective leaned forward in his seat. "Who in particular, do you want me to have spoken to? Could it perhaps be Reverend Edward Smith by any chance?"

The blanch was impossible to prevent as colour drained from Jayden's face. Now she had done it. "I guess so," she said quietly. "Reverend McLean often kept the curates late. It was his..." she tailed off.

"It was his what?" Lambert persisted.

Jayden stood up, pushing her seat backwards with her legs and turned to face the tinted window behind her. The detective was sharp though, not needing to see her eyes when he could read her body language.

"What was the vicar like, as a person?"

Jayden sighed. It was a logical question. "I'm sure there are better people able to answer that. I tended to avoid the man. He was bullish and antagonistic and treated his curates badly."

"Badly in what way?"

The slippery slope opened up unavoidably before Jayden. She had arrived in the very place that she had hoped to avoid. Thinking long and hard about her answer, Jayden remained with her back turned towards the detective. If she told him about the vicar's treatment of Ed, he was bound to jump to conclusions, especially if she added the small detail of their loud disagreement on the night the man died.

With no idea why she was so evasive, Jayden deflected the suspicion onto someone else. She turned around victoriously. "Brian, he treated Brian really badly. A few weeks ago, a client who hadn't been to church for a long time asked if we could go and sit in the pews for a while. She thought it might help her."

"Is that usual?" Lambert asked and Jayden cocked her head quizzically while she contemplated the question.

"Not really," she replied, "but we had been working on her phobia of being outside her home and it was what she wanted to do."

To Jayden's surprise, the detective let out a belly laugh which didn't quite fit with his professional air. "So with spider phobias, do you go poking around in the back of cupboards with clients, or bungee jumping with those afraid of heights?"

Lambert's smile died on his lips at the look of fury on Jayden's face. She walked around the desk to where he sat, standing over him with a flush to her cheeks and a new stiffness in her body. When she spoke, the detective could almost feel the acid dripping down his neck. "I'm so pleased that you find my clients hilarious, Officer Lambert. Perhaps *they* would be amused by your inability to commit to relationships, or a sense of dissatisfaction with what you have which makes you flirt with new opportunities. Why is it that the older detective rarely speaks to you or acknowledges you in a room? How does it make you feel to be underrated by someone whom you respect? We all have issues and difficulties Detective Lambert; the courage is in dealing with them."

Jayden walked over to the office door and wrenched it open. "I think our chat is over. Goodbye."

Chris Lambert was not only speechless; he was stunned. How was it that the woman had learned so much about him just from the minimal contact they had shared? He floundered in his chair but made no attempt to leave his position. He muttered something unintelligible as Jayden tapped the toe of her boot impatiently on the floor. Inwardly she fumed at the man's insensitivity towards damaged, hurting individuals but also at herself. It was wrong to utilise her knowledge of human behaviour to read him like that and worse still to use it against him. Consumed by her inner thoughts, she was surprised when hearing the squeak of the leather chair, she was met by the imploring eyes of the detective.

"I'm really sorry," he said contritely. "I shouldn't have made fun of them like that. How did you know...about me?"

Jayden let the fire door shut on its closer and came to sit back down at the desk. It seemed too good to be true that the detective was now the one on the back foot, negating her fumbled need to defend Ed. She observed him quietly. "The other day you were wearing a man's engagement ring and now you aren't.

You could have taken it off for a number of reasons, a sports game or because you had to. Only you keep rubbing at the spot where it was with a look of regret in your eyes. You have a way of flirting which leaves the other person to do the work if they are willing and that wouldn't happen if you were committed to the person who gave you the ring. The older detective, I'm sorry, I can't remember his name, treats you as though you aren't there. It's rude, but you haven't said anything as though you don't feel deserving of the elevation to your current post. It's simply that he just doesn't like you snapping at his heels and is threatened by you. I don't believe it's personal."

Jayden leaned forward. "I'm sure on a sliding scale, these issues would seem far worse than a frightened woman who asks to sit quietly in an empty church she once loved. But you see, she lost her soul mate a year ago in a car accident. The following week her home was invaded while she was in bed and she was beaten for the cost of a flat screen television and an old laptop computer. I'm sure I don't have to tell you about the kind of damage one human being inflicts on another for financial gain." The detective had the decency to look thoroughly ashamed. "That's why I will guard my clients' confidentiality with my life," Jayden said softly, "and you will not be getting access to the finer points of their misery without a search warrant."

Lambert nodded with understanding. But then he proved why he was already a detective at his young age. "What did the vicar do?" he asked shrewdly. "To Brian, the curate. What did he do while you were in the church?"

Jayden sat back and closed her eyes. The memory

was as perplexing as it was dreadful. There was no harm in sharing it however. "We sat down near the pillar towards the back of the pews. We both prayed for a while, which is possibly why the reverend didn't realise we were there. He appeared up near the line where the walls meet the roof and it was curious because only his head showed. I hadn't even realised there was a balcony up there; it's so well blended into the structure. He appeared to move around two whole sides of the nave and then stopped directly opposite us. To my surprise, he held a mug of something over the top of the balcony and poured liquid from it as though he was watering the garden. The vicar said nothing and walked back around the ceiling to wherever he had come from. It was truly astounding."

"Did your...client see?" Lambert asked, interested.

"No, thank goodness," Jayden replied. "She had her head down and her eyes closed praying. She looked up when she heard a splash but only saw the vicar retreating around the edge of the ceiling. She asked what had happened and I said I didn't know - because I didn't. How could I explain something like that?"

"So, are you telling me that Reverend Brian was underneath?" Lambert asked and his butt edged towards the front of his seat with anticipation.

"Well, that's the curious thing," Jayden answered, "I didn't even realise Brian was there until we were going through the doors at the altar end of the church. I had thought the vicar had just tipped his cup of tea over the balcony and I wanted to move in case he was going to walk round to our side and drop something on me. As I went through the door and looked back, Brian sat up in the pew. The poor man looked shocked and possibly burned. He seemed understandably devastated and wiped his face on his cardigan. For a moment there, I thought perhaps he was crying."

Lambert was all business as he made copious notes on his pad. Then he surprised Jayden further. "What do you know of a Mr..." he consulted his notes, "Macdonald?"

For a moment, Jayden floundered unsure of the name. It seemed vaguely familiar but not in a personal way. Her forehead creased in concentration and her green eyes narrowed, but she had to admit defeat finally, shaking her head and causing her long curls to bounce against her shoulders.

"Cecil and Beryl?" Lambert pressed and recognition flooded into Jayden's face.

"Yes, Beryl was the organist here for...well, forever actually. She was immensely talented." Jayden bit her lip. "I feel mean now, she's only been gone for a few months. I didn't use her surname; she was always just Beryl."

"What do you know of her husband?" Lambert asked. Jayden shrugged.

"Just that he's the nicest man. He wouldn't hurt a fly, if that's what you're asking. He's been a church warden for years, but I think he resigned shortly after his wife died.

"He's been suggested to us as someone who may have wanted the vicar dead. He was overheard threatening the reverend on Christmas Eve."

Jayden exhaled angrily. It never ceased to amaze her how quickly activated the human desire to share in trouble was. She wondered which of the 'concerned' congregation members had bleated to the cops about Cecil's distraught outburst after the *Carols by Candlelight* service. "He didn't *threaten* anyone," Jayden countered, with aggravation in her voice. "Reverend McLean said, somewhat tactlessly that he'd had to pay for an organist seeing as they no longer had one. He'd made no secret, either publicly or privately that poor Beryl's death had inconvenienced him greatly, but it was just a little too much for Cecil that evening. His son had persuaded him to come to the service, hoping that it might help to be somewhere that Beryl loved to be, but it was too much, too soon and he was overwhelmed. Reverend McLean actually suggested from the pulpit that folk be a little more generous than usual, seeing as the organist needed paying. Some people thought it was a joke and laughed, but Cecil approached him about it on his way out of the front."

"Were you there?" Lambert asked, frantically jotting. "Or is this hearsay?"

"I sat with Cecil and his son," Jayden said abruptly, growing progressively fed up with the game. Her elbow ached; her clients were struggling somewhere, unable to access her help because of the cordon around the church and she wanted to be at home, curled up on her sofa.

"What did Mr Macdonald do?" Lambert asked directly.

"Nothing initially. He just wanted to leave. But the rest of the congregation wanted to see him and wish him well, so he ended up trapped near the front doors. Reverend McLean usually stands...used to stand," Jayden corrected herself, "just inside the doors to shake hands with everyone. It was his way of ensuring that he was the centre of attention the whole way through the service, until the bitter end. Martin Macdonald tried to get his father out but inevitably, Reverend McLean made a beeline for him. To everyone's stunned amazement, he asked if Cecil would consider making a donation towards the cost of the organist."

Even Lambert found it hard to keep the disgust from creeping into his expression, curbing it quickly. "So, if I've got this right, he wanted the widower to stump up towards the cost of his dead wife's replacement?"

"Yep," Jayden sighed. "That's about it."

"Geez, no wonder the old guy lost his cool!"

"He didn't!" Jayden interjected crossly. "I don't know who you've been talking to but they've got a few facts wrong. Cecil held himself with complete dignity. It was his son, Martin, who..."

"Who what?"

Chris Lambert was sharp and too late, Jayden realised how once again she had been played. "It doesn't matter," she tried, "Martin didn't kill the vicar. He doesn't have it in him!"

"What did he say, Miss Mitchell?"

Jayden shifted uncomfortably in her seat. "Cecil was quite shaken and Martin was in the process of helping him out through the doors. He leaned into the vicar and said, 'You're going to get what's coming to you.' Then they left. I followed them out and helped Martin get his father into the front seat of his car. Cecil looked sick. But I promise you, Martin didn't do it."

Her voice sounded plaintive even to herself and it was unattractive and subordinate. *Guilt* accompanied a wave of sickness at the thought that she had exonerated Cecil and incriminated his son. "Look," she tried, her voice forcibly calm and placatory, "I spoke to Martin just after Christmas. He told me that it was all fine; his father had asked him just to let it go. Martin and his wife are members of a lovely little parish church out at Stow and Cecil had been there with them and loved it. It was fine; they were all moving on with their lives."

"The person I spoke to mentioned that the Macdonalds had a key to the church so that Mrs Macdonald could come and practice. What do you know about that?"

Jayden felt violently ill, to the point where she thought she might have to excuse herself and bolt for the ladies' toilet. In her head she could still hear the beautiful cresting waves of music, rising and falling in the cavernous church. Despite telling the detective previously that she and Cam rarely ventured into the main church, Jayden had forgotten the stolen moments of peace that she had enjoyed of an afternoon, stealing into the back pews to hear Beryl practice. She had been very gifted, crafting the music with angelically inspired digits and bringing Jayden much needed peace with every crashing or caressing note. "I don't know," her voice faltered. "Maybe Cecil gave the key back. How can they prove it now? He would have given it to McLean."

CHAPTER SEVENTEEN

"Ah fiancé," Raff's words stunned Jayden as Ed led her into the kitchen. Raff's brother had opened the front door with a gentle smile that made her heart flip over in her chest; his dark hair tousled from a recent shower. He had answered her knock so quickly that he had to have been on his way out of the front door, possibly delaying his exit in order to escort Jayden upstairs.

As Raff uttered his unfortunate greeting, Jayden felt Ed's eyes flick towards her. She stole a look sideways at him and saw the expression of disappointment and betrayal stamped across his face and knew that he was replaying what she had said the other night - that she had only recently been considering a relationship. He had got it wrong. It wasn't Raff who caused her heart to thud erratically when she saw him - and it wasn't Raff whose dark hair and Italian good looks she sought out with her searching eyes at church. *He's married!* She corrected herself again immediately for the twentieth time that day.

Raff came over and kissed her lovingly on the cheek. Jayden forced down the irritation which rose unbidden as he put an arm possessively around her, banging her cast in the process. She hissed and pulled herself free. "Ed told me about that," Raff said, eyeing it curiously. "Can I sign my name on it?"

Jayden shook her head. Nobody was going to write

anything on it. She hated seeing them that way, looking as offensive as a graffitied wall. The fleeting thought came to her that it wouldn't have killed him to have popped to see her, or to return her handbag. "I came to pick my handbag up," she said politely, but her tone was stilted and awkward. Ed seemed to have regained some of his composure and looked around the room.

"Did you leave it here? I haven't noticed it."

He cast around the work surfaces and under the table. Raff looked shifty.

"I know I left it here," Jayden pushed. "I need my work keys out of it. The cops are getting a warrant to look at my counselling notes."

"I know where it is," Raff stated, smiling as he went past her and thumped upstairs to the floor above. He returned from his bedroom holding her bag aloft, its dark leather strap bouncing insouciantly against his thigh.

"Why was it up there?" Jayden asked, feeling Ed's eyes boring into her. The atmosphere in the room had plummeted from welcoming to suspicious and something else that her alert senses failed to read.

"You must have left it there after I proposed to you."

Raff winked and gave Jayden a sultry look. The tension snapped with an almost audible ping and Ed jumped back into full control of his body. With an embarrassed wave of his hand, he smiled formally at Jayden and left the room, clearly giving them their privacy. Jayden looked at the back of his head wistfully as it bobbed quickly down the staircase and wondered what Raff was playing at.

"I've bought a ring," he said with childish

excitement, reaching into the cupboard above the hob. He looked smartly dressed in suit pants and a white shirt. Jayden looked at him incredulously. He was showing all the signs of psychological disturbance, or a person who had missed their Bipolar medication. He turned to her with the ecstatic face of a five-year-old, holding out a blue velvet box like it was his best picture, produced entirely for her with coloured crayons and finger paints.

"I...Raff...I..." she held her hand up, knowing as she did that it was pointless.

"I know you said you'd think about it," he crooned, coming across to her. Jayden was aware that she had said nothing of the kind. He continued, unperturbed, "I know that we'd be good together. The thing with Peter was just an interlude. That life isn't right for me. It's you I want."

He tried to kiss Jayden's open mouth and even the thought of it suddenly made her feel ill, as she caught sight of the naked desire in his eyes. But it was manufactured, unreal and pretence made the denial rawer. She was not what he wanted and never would be. But for Jayden, it was as though her heart had fixed itself to Ed and it would perceive anything else as adulterous. "No!" she pushed at his chest with both hands, her broken elbow jarring and smarting with the effort and force. Dreadful memories flashed across her vision and Raff's overwhelming personality made her feel as trapped as Wes' physicality had all those years ago. Panic welled up inside Jayden, spurred on by a sudden lack of control over her situation. *I have to be in control, I have to be in control*...the tape in Jayden's rational mind screamed out at her and she reacted, kicking Raff hard in the shins. The waiting spirit of *Fear* cackled gleefully and settled comfortably once again on her upturned face.

She had not yet taken off her boots and the impact was painful, dropping the man's glossy head forwards as Jayden swung her handbag strap and clouted him full in the face with the body of it. The velvet box flew gracefully across the room, landing on the other side of the table and with a second's worth of guilt, Jayden fled yet again, clattering down the stairs and out of the front door.

This time she used the back streets of Lincoln, running headlong down Michaelgate, Hungate and doubling back on herself through Motherby Lane before the High Street took her home. It was perilously steep and treacherous, but she managed somehow, arriving at her front door with her frightened breath coming in heaves and her legs trembling underneath her. Two men covertly watched her struggle with the front door key from around her neck, seeing her bend almost double to fit it into the lock without taking it off its string. One sat calmly on a bench and the other observed from further up the high street, puffing slightly from his exertion and the concern which writhed in the pit of his stomach for her.

Once inside, Jayden slammed the door on the world and went upstairs to her sanctuary, to lick her emotional wounds and wonder how the men in her circles always seemed to be her undoing.

It was only later, with a glass of wine valiantly in her good hand that she dared to open her handbag, finding her mobile phone without charge and her keys isolated in the bottom. The bunch looked to be intact, the filing cabinet key looking tiny against the office

Yale and the front door mortise to the counselling suite's badly fitting front doors. It wasn't a particularly big bunch, hanging from a ladybird key ring that her mother had bought her when she visited Aberystwyth last. It was probably that fact that alerted Jayden to the different look and feel about them, which on further examination, showed that the front door key to her flat was definitely missing.

CHAPTER EIGHTEEN

Jayden hardly slept. Knowing that someone else had a key to her safe house was utterly petrifying. The demons fluttered around the flat, determined to regain their foothold in Jayden's life. But she was not alone in the spiritual realm and other divine spirits went into battle on her behalf as she lay sleepless in her bed.

Because her mistress couldn't settle, neither could Nahla. She slunk around the flat, bouncing Jayden out of bed and then getting underfoot. She tried to convince her mistress that she was starving hungry by running over to the fridge, staring hopefully and winding her way back again, snaking her tail round Jayden's bare legs like silk caresses. Jayden fixed a fleece around her shoulders and stepped outside onto the roof garden around five in the morning, so that the cat could go outside and annoy the city night creatures for sustenance. "Find your own breakfast, girl," Jayden muttered into the darkness.

She stayed outside until her fingers and toes were almost frozen, enjoying the way that the bitter air iced the pain in her bones and stopped the agonising pounding emanating from inside the cast. The nurse in Emergency had said that it would throb, but knowing that fact didn't lessen the pain it caused when it did.

Jayden leaned her forehead against the balcony rail and let her brain run through its list of fears, tired of battling with her mind for it to be still. Her primary concern was the whereabouts of her front door key. Nick's presence had rattled her understandably and he was an unlikely murderer for the vicar, but even less likely pilferer of her door key. It seemed that he'd had little opportunity to do either. Raff had been weird about her handbag, but distracted by the bizarre family unit which he was happily constructing in his head. It seemed unlikely that he had her door key. Jayden cringed as she thought about his happiness over the ring he bought her, the excitement leaking out of his face and his sparkling eyes catching up with the guilt she felt at her treatment of him. Perhaps without meaning to, Jayden had led him on. Like Wes. *No! Not like Wes!* Jayden chastised herself heavily. It was a familiar route filled with glass shards of blame underfoot and she had no intention of going there. Not today.

Ed could have easily killed the vicar. He had motive and opportunity, yet her mind was an unwilling participant in the reasoning process for that scenario, rejecting every related spark of thought and Jayden gave up even considering it with any seriousness. He wouldn't be a killer because she didn't *want* him to be. It was that simple. Brian was clearly inept, which put him handily outside the realms of suspicion. He had suffered under McLean for years and baulked at action through his own impotence. Surely if he were going to kill the vicar for ill-treatment, he would have done it aeons ago.

Cecil and Martin Macdonald were obviously in the frame, by dint of a possibility that they still owned a key to the church. But as Jayden considered it against the backdrop of what she knew about either of them, the idea grew more ludicrous. She realised sadly that they were only suspects because she had made them such and *Guilt* swooped down and knotted its ugly fingers through her hair as it settled its greasy rump on the crown of Jayden's head. She let her forehead sink onto her good arm along the balcony rail and listened to her cat make short work of killing a couple of mice in the guttering above her flat. The irritating voice in her head reminded her that Ed was the most likely person with both motive and opportunity. Not wanting to think about that particular possibility, Jayden went back indoors and tried to block out the voice.

A familiar sound captured Jayden's attention around six in the morning. It was a tiny noise, just the scraping of a metal key in the lock, but it caused her heart to stop for a second and then resume thudding in an adrenaline fuelled thump. She was slumped on the sofa in the living room area, swaddled in a blanket watching breakfast television begin to start. The delighted faces of the presenters masked tiredness, family problems and personal issues under the layers of makeup and bonhomie.

Jayden muted the TV and listened again at the top of the stairs which led down to the street, trying to discern the tiny sound through the swishing of the blood in her ears. The door handle tipped as the person pushed against the jamb. Whoever it was had successfully unlocked it, but failed to take account of the bolts at the top and bottom that kept it closed against them. On an impulse, Jayden hurried quietly up the spiral stairs, wrenching open the sliding doors of her bedroom and scuttling out onto the roof garden in her bare feet. The front wall of the balcony was slightly back from the edge of the roof below. It had apparently been part of the planning regulations so as not to spoil the upwards view from the ancient street. Jayden reached over, banging her cast against the rail at the top and peering into the dark, lamp-lit street below while her bare toes stuck to the frozen surface beneath them.

Her view began about six feet into the street; the rest impeded by window sills and the set-back nature of the balcony. Further up the street someone was running and she could hear the steady slap of their training shoes. Frantic now she peered into the gloom, feeling vulnerable and fighting the urge to run down and out into the street to satiate her curiosity.

A dark head appeared in the middle of the street moving north and a body clad in fluro running gear. She recognised the male, but in the poor visibility could not distinguish which of the Abbadeli brothers it was. Her heart filled with misgiving and misery. It was logical. One of *them* must have taken her key. Jayden went back inside and closed the doors into her room. Nahla was delighted with the short interlude as she had managed to catch a mouse and was in the process of scoffing it on the bathroom floor. Jayden sighed and went to clear the mess up, mistrust filling her momentarily tender heart and sealing it over with spiritual concrete.

Lily McGowan fought against the filling of the hard-won cracks as the higher power shook its head and refused to be beaten.

CHAPTER NINETEEN

"Absolutely no way! I don't have time today." Jayden backed towards her office door. She didn't counsel rape victims. Rita had told her repeatedly that she should, believing that she was truly ready. Despite having passed her degree with flying colours, the scenarios relating to sexual abuse had been the hardest to deal with and Jayden had employed a very effective mask to protect herself from feeling emotions that threatened her equilibrium. She had done multiple hours of supervised counselling as part of her qualification, keeping it all at arm's length through an act of pure will and fooling herself that it was all 'pretend' for the benefit of her degree. It had kept her sane and allowed her to fly under Rita's capable radar and hopefully the poor women and girls she had encountered had not been cheated by Jayden's detachment.

But she hadn't been quite as clever as she had thought and the whole thing caught her up twice without warning during her course, biting her hard when she felt least able to cope. A couple of times in her final year, Jayden had crashed spectacularly and needed to take sick leave. She knew inwardly that it wasn't a great way to deal with things but despite years of head knowledge and watching existences changed through exposure of the demons in peoples' lives, Jayden would have to face something insurmountable in order to recover fully from her ordeal. She knew in her heart that it wasn't possible. It would kill her for sure.

Jayden had been taught that sexual trauma was like a bag of frozen peas. Snap frozen on the day that they were picked; the peas could be pulled out of the freezer years later and have kept their freshness. That was how it was for a rape victim. Noises, smells, words, voices, even another person's physical appearance could pull the peas from the freezer of their mind and the experience would be just as fresh, equally as painful, undimmed by the passage of time or the dulling of the original physical trauma. Inwardly, that was what Jayden was afraid of, that someone else's misery would have the potential to yank her back in time, force her again to face the nightmares and the flashbacks. Each time she thought that she had dealt with it all, back it would come. She had stopped counting how often she had faced her own demons, knowing only that she couldn't cope with another visit into her past.

There had, fortunately, been only a few abuse cases in the past five years of working at the centre and those, Jayden had been able to sidestep neatly, brushing off the guilt and justifying her selfishness as Cam dealt with them or referred them on. But today was not Jayden's lucky day and Sal greeted her with a look of urgency as her snowy boots landed on the mat just inside the front door.

"I've moved your first appointment. I hope you won't be cross, but I really need you to see this young girl. It's urgent. They don't want Cam; they want you." Sal's jaw flexed, the line of bone and teeth showing underneath the skin of her slender face as she contemplated the counsellor.

"I can't. Not today." Nobody else in the tiny practice was aware of anything relating to Jayden's past because she kept it so effectively to herself, allowing only what she wished to project to be at the forefront of her image. But she was aware that the high colour induced by the bracing winter walk to work had drained from her face almost instantaneously and her shoulders had visibly sagged. Jayden felt brittle and two-dimensional, as though the smallest puff of wind would blow her away. With everything in her being, she wished for that breeze and the escape it promised.

Ed appeared in the reception with an A4 piece of paper. He looked fresh and clean, his olive skin glowing healthily against the sombreness of his clothing. Jayden fought the urge to run to him, remembering his safe, strong arms around her. But the picture was quickly overwritten by the memory of the figure running back up the High Street in the dark. Disappointment coursed through her; a familiar betrayal reflex and she considered quitting right now and just not returning.

Ed laid the paper carefully on Sal's desk and gave the receptionist a cursory nod, acknowledging that she understood what it was. Then both of them looked at Jayden, transfixed on the doormat, her face a mask of horror.

"Jayden?" Sal was speaking to her. In fact, she had been saying words for some moments, none of which had penetrated Jayden's consciousness. Ed let go of the paper and looked towards Jayden with an expression of genuine consternation. Jayden managed to collect herself enough to unlock her office and disappear inside.

She leaned back against the knotted wood, feeling its solidity underneath her hands and the back of her head. *"No, no, no!"*

The gentle knocking vibrated against her body and caused her heart to restart properly. Blood surged through her body like an adrenaline rush and it was not pleasant. "Go away!"

Jayden moved back from the door and began to undo her coat buttons with shaking hands. Ed turned the handle and entered without an invitation, catching her as she lifted her coat off her shoulders and struggled to release the cast. The sling had been left at home, more a hindrance than a help. Ed's strong, capable fingers disengaged the edge of the plaster from the cuff of Jayden's coat. "Nice run this morning?" she asked him bitingly and he nodded slowly.

"Yes thanks." He looked confused.

Jayden turned away from his confirmation and drew in a deep breath as she sought oxygen and energy. To her surprise, Ed adjusted her clients' chair and plonked his lean, muscular body down in it. Jayden bought herself time, fiddling to put her coat on a coat hanger and slide it into the built-in closet in the corner of the room. "I need to talk to you about a young girl coming in soon. She's fifteen, goes to another church in the south of the city and her parents called me late yesterday. They need help. She was raped a few weeks ago and they don't know where to turn..."

"Victim Support," Jayden said without feeling, her voice as cold as her chilling heart. "They'll take her."

"She won't talk to them, but her family know your supervisor and she's convinced the girl to talk to you."

Bloody Rita! "No," Jayden said with force. *"No!"*

She was guarded and wooden and the curate displayed infinite patience and consideration towards her, despite the fact that the woman in front of him hissed and spat like a feral cat. "When you said that you'd had a bad experience..."

"I'm not discussing this with *you*," Jayden said spitefully, putting all the misery at his deception into her voice. He had stolen her key and tried to gain entry into her safe place, when all he had to do was knock on the door. Perhaps that was the problem; if he had asked, she would have let him in willingly.

Ed rose slowly and eyeballed Jayden uncomfortably, causing her pale skin to blush uncontrollably. "She's called Clara and she's on her way in with her very distraught parents. This is the first time she has voluntarily left the house and I'm *telling* you to see her. For the love of God Jayden, we all have to do things we don't like. You can help this child, so do it!"

Ed pitied Jayden as she flapped and flailed in her seat, squirming like someone who'd been stung by a jellyfish. He walked decisively round to her side of the desk and pulled her to her feet roughly, ignoring the frenzied resistance. Jayden's innate reaction was to hit out at him, but her heart overruled it and she found herself crushed into his masculine chest, his deodorant and aftershave filling her nostrils as she took deep breaths. "Everything will be ok," he whispered, sliding his hands up the side of her neck and into her hair. "It feels right. It has to be you. It will be ok, I promise, I will pray for you. I'll go to the vestry right now and do that for you and I won't stop until you're through."

He released her, calm now and kissed the side of her forehead slowly, tenderly as though he meant it. All feeling of betrayal and aggression at his deception over the door key seemed numbed and inconsequential as though Jayden had been put under a spell. "I'll get Sal to let me know when she's gone and then I'll come for you. The whole time that she's in this room, I will be praying for you. *Trust me.*"

He looked back at her as his hand rested momentarily on the door handle. She reminded him of a daisy as she sat in her chair; her forehead leaned desperately on her good hand. She was a picture of dismay; a beautiful flower propped up by a delicate, fragile stem, given only the shortest of hours to bloom and delight. It almost broke his heart. Sal's knock was tentative and Ed wrested the door open and greeted her with a smile that didn't reach his eyes.

The child and her parents sat in the reception area, each a bag of nerves for different reasons, each utterly poleaxed by circumstance.

"Mr and Mrs Schofield. Clara." Ed's voice was pleasant and reassuring as he greeted the little broken family. Sal strode quickly across the room to Jayden, laying the white sheets of paper on the desk in front of her.

"They signed a contract and the little girl's filled in the initial counselling form. Ed drove it out to them last night. Shall I send them in?" Sal was concerned at the misery and self-doubt which leaked out of Jayden's eyes and tried to smile reassuringly at her. "You've helped heaps of people in this community. They all love you. You'll be great."

She turned on her heel, her bobbed hair swinging

jauntily and her long skirt tinkling against the buckle on her boots. Jayden got shakily to her feet and walked to the door, as though bracing herself for the hangman's noose. She arrived in the reception area, astounded at what she found there.

It was the face of the girl's mother who turned to her first. Grey-faced and gaunt, the unfortunate woman looked as though she hadn't slept in weeks. She probably hadn't. Tears threatened at the edges of her soft brown eyes like an overfilled reservoir. It would take the smallest inconsequential piece of minutiae to set the flood in motion, destroying everything in its noisy path. But the father's face was agony to behold. *Grief* and *Desolation* soared around his head, digging their nasty faces into his and screaming, 'useless' at him, compounding his feelings of failure for being unable to protect his little girl. The teenager had been violated, but her family were being endlessly tortured.

Jayden shook hands with them all, Clara included, fleetingly hoping that they didn't notice the clamminess of her touch. Then they all sat down in the comfortable square of seating that made up the reception area. Ed sat close to Jayden, so close that she could feel his trouser clad leg through her skirt. It instilled comfort into her and something told her that he was already interceding for her.

"I would like to see Clara for a while by herself," Jayden began, noticing the sense of relief which crossed the teenager's delicate features. "We should be finished in about an hour, so if you would like to go to the tea rooms around the other side of the church, or go for a walk..."

John Schofield rose quickly to his feet. "No," he

said assertively, "we're all in this together. You need to see us all."

Jayden took a deep breath in, but it was Ed who came to her rescue. "I agree with Miss Mitchell actually. I think she needs to assess Clara alone. You don't have to leave the building; the tea rooms are an integral part of the church extension. I could use a coffee so I'll walk through with you." Ed stood up and indicated with his hand that they should follow him. Both parents were understandably reluctant, needing to provide a human shield for their precious child against further hurt. Mr Schofield looked as though he would protest again, but Ed's reassuring face convinced him.

They both kissed their little girl and promised that they wouldn't be far away. She smiled, a tight action which appeared more like a grimace. Ed showed them down the corridor which joined the elderly church building to the counselling rooms, turning off before the back entrance to the nave. Jayden was hit with the sudden realisation that he had promised to go into his vestry and pray for her. She knew without a doubt that she needed him to. A single glance back in her direction from his stunning blue eyes was enough to communicate wordlessly to her, that it didn't matter where he was. A promise was a promise and he was not a man who broke them often.

Back in her office, Jayden didn't sit behind her desk. She pulled the second visitors' chair up at right angles to Clara's and grabbed her clipboard, giving the child a moment to adjust to her surroundings while Jayden read the childish scrawl on the initial counselling form. It made sad reading. Clara couldn't sleep, needing medication to doze at best, hadn't eaten properly since it had happened, cried uncontrollably without warning and felt as though her body hurt all over, all of the time.

Jayden bit her lip and smiled at the tiny child adjacent to her. She had beautiful blonde hair which tumbled unkempt down her back. Starvation had made her skinny and her bones showed through at the wrist. It had caused her face to look tight and skeletal, huge brown eyes shining out, now far too big for the tiny visage.

Jayden opened her mouth to speak, but to her surprise was beaten to it by the girl. "Aunty Rita recommended you. Nobody else in the family knows. Dad rang her yesterday and she said it had to be you. She told him you'd understand."

Jayden put her hand over her eyes, shielding her from the child's hopeful expression. Inwardly she used every awful curse word about Rita that she had ever heard, shoving a few of them God's way while she was at it. *How dare she? Damn Rita! She had no right!*

Peace flooded her soul suddenly, setting her world back upright on its axis and a strange feeling of relief came over her. *Be honest.* The words came to her as though spoken out loud and Jayden looked up amazed, to meet the searching eyes of the girl staring at her. "Yes Clara," she replied. "I do know exactly what you're going through. Perhaps we need to walk out of this mess together. How would you feel about that?"

Clara sighed as freedom folded her body backwards into the leatherette seat cushions. Her tiny emaciated frame seemed to shudder and sag with its momentary reprieve. "I'd like that very much," she whispered.

It wasn't professional and it certainly wasn't usual. The training manual or the lecture had no format for a counsellor who held the hand of a suffering child and cried with her, as she described the attack. Jayden felt the searing pain between her own legs again and the crushing of her slender windpipe, crying silently, big, swollen tears plopping onto the seat with a dull thud. Clara's story didn't have to be pulled or plied from her, it gushed and burst without release until it was all out in the airwaves, polluting them and healing her. The sons of *Death* swooped about the room, filled with glee at the recounting of the child's horror but somehow sensed that their days were numbered.

"Tell me what happened to you," Clara begged as Jayden handed her another tissue.

"Not today," Jayden said softly. "Today is all about you." She smiled and the little girl smiled back, the radiant beam of one who has spotted the broken bolt through the keyhole of her prison door and knows that release is imminent.

"When you think about the situation as a whole," Jayden asked, "what's the very worst part of it? What is the one thing that keeps you awake at night, and strips away your hunger?"

Clara blew her nose noisily and thought for a moment. But her answer was not in the least what Jayden had expected. Surely it should have been the invasive police procedures, checking for AIDS, infection, pregnancy, the rape act itself and the powerlessness of the victim, the indignity, the humiliation, but it was none of these things.

"It was the look on Dad's face when he got to the police station," Clara said, shedding another willing crop of dreadful tears. "He looked destroyed and a voice in my head said, *you caused that*. That was the very worst part."

Jayden tried to halt the enormous intake of breath that threatened to blow her body wide open. It didn't seem to want to stop coming, in and in and in it came. Fortunately, Clara chose that moment to try and get her nose under control and Jayden's difficulties were masked by the dribbly sounds of a never-ending-nose-excavation.

Guilt fluttered in front of Jayden's face in all its ugliness. It giggled uncontrollably with delight at her suffering and clapped its gnarly hands with glee at the thought of her complete destruction. It would keep both females from everything that was good and pleasing, all the delights that their Maker had designed them for. When they contemplated the marvelousness of their intricate female parts, they would not consider the joy of a loved partner or the birth of their child. For them would be the memory of their abuse, their futile struggles and the pain of violation. Its sickening silent laughter was only halted by the counsellor speaking out its name. "*Guilt.*"

Clara looked up, her tissue soggy and pitiful in her long delicate fingers. She looked questioningly at Jayden, whose breath seemed to release like a deflated airbed, slowly, quietly and without fuss. "It's the guilt that is the worst," Jayden qualified. "We were Daddy's little girls and wanted him to see the best in us. There's a shadow that crosses their eyes when they see what's happened and have to face what we've become. It's like the going out of a light. I agree." She looked across at Clara's red-rimmed eyes. "It is the worst part of all."

Clara's face broke into a watery smile. She had

pretty teeth, straight and attractive. She was a beautiful teenager and was going to be a stunning young woman. Jayden knew that the journey ahead would not be by the book. It would be unchartered, dangerous and beset by hazards at present unseen. But they would do it together. Jayden turned further in her seat, her clipboard and her notes forgotten, but the need to impart this one piece of wisdom into the girl, uppermost in her mind.

"You were not responsible for what someone else chose to do to you, so do not take responsibility for any of the consequences either. You are not responsible for your father's disappointment, or his anguish or his grief. Those belong to him and he will deal with them. Let them go and you'll find your burden lighter. *I release you*."

"Thank you," Clara smiled.

Both women mopped themselves up and Jayden finished the session. She asked Clara to do some homework before their next meeting. The teenager had to find ten things about herself that hadn't changed despite the attack. She could still be pretty, have nice hair and be good at maths. The rapist had already taken enough from her. Jayden would prevent him from stealing anymore.

As Clara reached up to hug Jayden before she had fully grasped the door handle, *Guilt* let out a roar of fury and disappeared in a puff of smoke. Clara squeezed Jayden tight, but it was not the kind of contact that screamed of life rafts or gripping on to a solid object for dear life. It was to offer, as much as to receive, comfort, understanding and solidarity. Jayden held her in return and forgave herself for allowing this client to cause her to step outside her professional walls and knew inwardly that it would be all right.

Outside in reception, Clara's parents waited anxiously for their child to return. They expected the wasted husk who had gone in but were gratified by the teenager who emerged. Jayden shook their hands again and took the opportunity of an empty room, but for Sal, to suggest kindly that they each made appointments to see Campion. "I'd quite like to see *you*," Clara's mother said, with a hint of rejection in her voice. Jayden caught the look of dismay on the girl's face and shook her head kindly.

"I think that it would confuse my care of Clara," Jayden said. "It would be better for all of you to see separate people. You can go together or alone, it's entirely up to you. But Cam is the best, I can assure you."

They nodded resignedly and went over to make appointments with Sal, clearly at the 'try anything' stage of their crisis. Clara looked at her counsellor with a wan smile on her fragile face and to Jayden's surprise, winked. "*That's* what Aunty Rita said about you," she whispered, and followed her parents over to Sal's desk to book her own follow-up session in three days' time.

CHAPTER TWENTY

Jayden felt drained. After she had waved the family goodbye, she went back to her office and slumped into her chair behind the big wooden desk. She suddenly seemed to have so much to process.

Her father's smiling face wafted across her inner vision, his full head of greying hair, often stuffed underneath a woolly hat as he went off to check his herd of prized sheep. Hannah had knitted a new hat every year and they were often misshapen, strange creations. Dan had pulled them on and pretended that he loved them, just to please her, no matter how weird they looked. Hannah still knitted them, only now, she no longer knew why. May took them down to a local homeless shelter and other men wore the wonky, pom-pommed affairs.

Jayden had spent seventeen years of her life in no doubt that he adored her; she was his little girl and never a day had gone by without him telling her how beautiful she was or how precious. He had been a good Christian man, who loved his wife and two children. They had been the perfect family.

His face as he had burst into the dingy squat in Bradford had been a mixture of anger and horror. His revered son had been slumped in a corner of the downstairs room, drooling as a needle dangled precariously from a vein in his bare foot. The heroin was contaminated enough to cause him instant health problems, but not to wipe him entirely off the face of the cursed carpet on which he had appeared to be little more than a wasted mound of clothing. Alerted to his child's muffled screams of pain, Dan's feet had led him instantly to the filthy upstairs room.

Jayden ran her hand over her eyes, smudging the remainder of her makeup as she squeezed the bridge of her nose to prevent further tears leaking out. Her father's face had been aghast with shock. It was as though he had held his breath in abject horror, not quite understanding at first what he was seeing. Wes had Jayden's throat in his hand, pressing down mercilessly in his excitement. His other hand gripped a steel switchblade, already open and stained with blood. Her school skirt had been up around her waist and her face a blank, staring mask of fear. It had been a paralysing sight for a father. A school skirt was a childish, carefree thing, a pleated, tartan representative of girlishness. It didn't belong there in that place. It should have been no part of that act. But then nor should his beautiful daughter.

Dan had acted without thinking, seizing the rapist by his hair and his open shirt collar and throwing him off his daughter. Jayden was bleeding from the sex but also from a stab wound under her ribs, which Wes had used to silence her cries. He preferred the whores who worked for him to stay quiet and at least pretend to like his efforts. The knife had slipped in a little deeper than he had intended, but he would have no further use for the girl after this, so it made no odds to him.

An uncharacteristic red mist had descended over the gentle father's mind and he had displayed a furious temper, kicking Wes hard in the groin and making the man double over in pure agony, doing irreparable damage and putting out his fire once and for all. The steel toe caps of Dan's work boots had broken Wes' eye socket and decimated three ribs, driving the dope dealer and part-time pimp nearer to the floor to slobber and cry. Dan had knelt and scooped his daughter up into his arms, pulling her torn skirt back down over her dignity with tenderness and care. "My beautiful daughter," he had said, the words catching in his throat. Jayden had looked up into his face, unable to read the myriad expressions there and had been staring into his disbelief through her tear filled eyes, when the wide-eyed look of realisation had crossed his features.

Wes' face appeared above him, writhing in discomfort with his own injuries and speckling blood over her father's white-shirted shoulder. The long bladed knife was slipped into Dan's body through his back, puncturing his left lung and wrecking his insides. But the father wasn't yet done and the last thing Wes remembered before waking up in the hospital under guard was the feel of Dan's fist in his face. The action of turning caused the blade to touch the finer workings of the honourable man's heart, jamming itself inside one of the precious cavities and severing a splendid career as a father. Despite his injuries, Dan still managed to set his daughter carefully on the ground, before keeling over onto the stained floorboards.

It all happened so quickly, fast forwarding Dan's exit as though *Death* was in a hurry to claim his soul. With no mobile phone and no landline in the dirty derelict house, Jayden had sobbed as the life dripped from her father. She had just enough time to apologise over and over for something she had convinced herself was her fault. "Sorry Daddy, sorry."

Her father's blood had mingled and diluted itself in hers as his final juddering breath left his body and she had cradled his head in her soiled, bloody lap.

In his haste, Dan had run two red traffic lights and fortunately been seen by a passing police car. Slow to make the turn they had lost him as he flew after his son's tail lights. Nick had nosed his vehicle down a steep driveway, effectively making himself invisible as he dragged Jayden into the property via the back door. Dan had driven frantically around and finally abandoned his 4 x 4 truck slewed across the road and the top of the driveway. Cruising around in their search the cops had come upon the truck with its engine still idling and ventured inside to search the property, night sticks drawn and back up already on its way.

The blood bath in front of them had been horrific. Mistaking Jayden for one of the local prostitutes, they had not been as attentive as they should and her stab wound was initially missed. It was only the kindly ambulance man, a little more experienced than the policemen who were equipped mostly with the blind enthusiasm of the young, who pried Dan's head from Jayden's lap and noticed the flow of blood that continued to soak the school skirt. Wes' state of undress and the finger marks around her throat, already turning shades of black and blue, gave the game away and Jayden was treated differently from that moment on.

It was only when the three blood-soaked creatures, plus one drugged up comatose male, were ambulanced to the hospital and Jayden's mother arrived to identify three of them as hers that the full extent of the horror was finally understood. Jayden's spleen was removed in surgery and by the time she was awake enough fully to comprehend the dire state of her circumstances, most of the action was over. Her father was dead, her brother was under arrest and Wes was undergoing surgery for a blood clot to his warped excuse for a brain. Jayden had lain in the hospital, flanked by Hannah's faithful presence and resigned herself to the fact that she would never recover. The demons had settled on her then, when at her most vulnerable she had failed to lock her soul against their lies and they had kept her prisoner ever since.

In masking her true feelings during her training and the subsequent five years of work, Jayden had denied Lily and played into the vile hands of the ghouls who held her hostage. She wiped her eyes again and wondered what life would be like from now on. She could feel more of her old self stirring in her heart and responded to it reluctantly.

A sharp rap on the door heralded Ed, as promised. He grabbed her coat from the closet and held out his hand to her. "Come."

Like a child, Jayden allowed him to lead her from the room, attempting to lock the door behind them and fumbling so badly that Ed had to take the key from her. With a wave at Sal and a raised eyebrow, he exited the centre, dragging his partner with him. He had already asked Sal to cancel Jayden's appointments for the day. The world would have to manage without her.

On the crazy paved path at the side of the church, he stripped off his white dog-collar, the mark of his trade and opened the top button of his black shirt.

Stuffing the stiff white thing in his jacket pocket, he tucked Jayden's uninjured right arm underneath his and led her gently as though out for a stroll.

The two detectives were just entering the side gates to make their way around to the counselling centre. The older man waved a slip of paper in their faces and told them victoriously that he had gotten a warrant from a justice of the peace. Jayden ignored them both completely, allowing herself to be led along by Ed, almost cracking a smile as she heard his reply to them in a jovial tone, "Jolly good."

The policemen stood and watched the odd pair turn the corner before shrugging at each other and proceeding into the building. Only Ed and Jayden had keys to the offices and only Jayden held the key to the precious filing cabinet. Both key holders were long gone by the time the deflated cops had debated the issue with an indignant Sal at the front desk. Campion appeared at his office doorway, following a client to the reception desk and read the warrant with a serious expression. It gave the detectives the power to search his office and cabinets also. He smiled and held the door open for them, whilst pointing out that even if they broke the door down into Jayden's office, the filing cabinet was bolted to the floor and tamper proof. "You would be better off waiting for her."

Ed walked Jayden out of the front gates and into the High Street. Her boot heels clacked on the pavement, resounding peculiarly off the three storey buildings all around them. Jayden was grateful that Ed didn't take her to the church cafe. Staffed by volunteers it was generally a lovely place to sit and waste some time but it could also be a hotbed of scintillating gossip. Coffee with the stand-in-vicar would be sure to arouse unhealthy interest in their companionship and almost definitely get back to Ed's wife.

They went instead to a small cafe tucked between two shops at the start of the pedestrian area. It was modelled on an Italian theme and Ed seemed at home there. The young girl behind the counter was somewhat smitten with his dark good looks and he bantered kindly with her for a moment while he ordered the drinks. Jayden skulked into the toilets to clean herself up. She hadn't grabbed her handbag and so was forced to scrub off the offending mascara using damp toilet roll but as the quality of the paper was not high, ended up covered in tiny threads of grey paper. The more water she used, the worse it got.

Jayden emerged eventually, feeling embarrassed about her blotchy red raw face and puffy eyes, but Ed glanced up from the newspaper he was perusing and appraised her warmly. Jayden felt the heat of attraction rising up inside her chest and fought to beat it down again. *After almost nine years of enforced drought, trust her to fall for a married one!*

Their drinks arrived and Ed smiled up nicely at the barista, who coloured slightly at his attention before returning to hide behind her noisy coffee machine and peek over the top at him longingly. The girl eyed Jayden with open curiosity, making her feel self-conscious and unworthy of being with the gorgeous man who was at that moment, stirring a sachet of sugar into his coffee. He did everything precisely, with concentration and a hint of perfectionism. His fingers were long and slender with a dusting of dark hair on the backs of his hands. His nails were clean and short, a healthy line of white along the edges showing that he wasn't a nail biter.

Without considering what the consequences might be, Jayden reached out the fingers of her right hand and touched the back of Ed's as he twirled the spoon in a rhythmic motion. He placed the object carefully on the table and met Jayden's fingers with his. There was a moment of intensity, as though the world had paled into insignificance around them while his fingers explored hers, knitting themselves through them as though designed to fit with surprising perfection. He turned her cool, smooth hand over and raised it to his mouth, kissing her curled digits tenderly. Feeling the eyes of the other customers straying their way, Jayden gently pulled her hand back and used the distraction of sipping her coffee to mask any awkwardness.

Ed seemed genuinely disappointed but covered it well, returning his attention to his drink, a cappuccino with an incredibly generous sprinkling of chocolate. "You like chocolate?" Jayden asked, suddenly tired of the silence, even though it wasn't overly oppressive. Ed leaned in conspiratorially.

"Not that much really. But the young lady behind the counter thinks I do."

Jayden bit her lip and tried not to look across at the barista. "Why don't you go to another cafe?" she asked, thinking it logical. Ed sighed and leaned back in his chair, looking around at the stonewashed walls and stencilled Roman pots. It oozed a kind of stereotypical Italy, which probably bore no relation to the reality.

"I like it here," he replied loyally, "it reminds me of home."

Jayden smiled in response and studied him

covertly from underneath her lashes. Ed felt her gaze and stayed deliberately still and quiet. It was a little like lying on the ground waiting for a nervous deer to sniff him out, running the risk of falling foul of its hooves or deceptively dangerous antlers. Jayden spoke suddenly, appealing for his wisdom and it made him feel as though he could take on the war-torn and raging world.

"What shall I do about giving the cops access to my notes?" she asked and Ed thought for a moment.

"I don't see that you have a choice. Their warrant effectively unlocks that filing cabinet, whether you like it or not. Why?"

Jayden lowered her voice. "If I tell you something, you have to keep it to yourself don't you? Because of the oath you swore when you became a curate."

Ed winced visibly and nodded slowly. "Kind of, but like you, there are certain circumstances that allow me to break that. I think you just need to tell me, Jayd."

"Well," she leaned forwards conspiratorially and he did likewise, their fringes meeting over the top of their coffees. "What if I told you that the notes from one of my clients could seriously implicate them in the vicar's murder?"

Ed let out a low whistle. "I'd say that was a real praline."

"What?" Jayden was confused.

"Oh sorry," Ed whispered with a smirk, "I have to swear in chocolate. The congregation doesn't much like their curates dropping the 'f-bomb' in church. Habit, sorry."

"This is serious, Ed! A woman's life could hang in the balance over this."

"Do you think she did it?" he asked in a whisper.

"Heck no!" came Jayden's retort. "She's crippled with arthritis and couldn't have even got up those stairs, let alone chucked her husband off the balcony. But if anyone had motive and opportunity, then it was her."

Ed's eyes widened and Jayden clapped her hand over her mouth. She had given everything away to this man, having fallen into the depths of his smouldering blue eyes and broken all of her own rules. He could see her inwardly beating herself up and didn't want that for her. Ed reached out and reclaimed her right hand, holding it tightly in his with no intention of letting her go. "I'm not going to say anything if you don't think she did it. But let's just talk this through properly. Are you saying that you've been treating the vicar's wife?"

Jayden nodded miserably. "Yes. Sal has to leave at four on a Thursday and Campion has a tutorial with the students he takes up at the university then. So she's been coming in to see me for the last six months. I just make sure that Sal leaves it free for me and she sneaks through. It's been fine up until now. Nobody needed to know."

"Can you tell me what you've been treating her for?" Ed asked gently, refusing to let Jayden's hand go so that she could scratch her nose. She was forced to use the other hand and caught the edge of her cast on her cheekbone. She gave a huge sigh and seemed reluctant, capitulating eventually.

"Anger management."

"Turkish delight!" Ed's response had a vaguely comic feel, despite the inappropriateness of it.

"Ed! Be serious!" she snapped at him again and he

bit his bottom lip.

"Sorry!" he whispered back. "What I really want to say is *bollocks, shit and bugger*, but it's not really on, is it?"

"No," Jayden shook her head. "But they're my sentiments exactly."

"So you think that the minute they start reading her notes, they'll be running the lights and two tones to arrest her?"

"Well, wouldn't you if you were them?" Jayden asked. "The thing is...her notes aren't actually in that filing cabinet. They're in my closet back at the office. I've hidden them up under the Christmas decorations. I know it's all a bit unethical, but I didn't want to run the risk of having that odious little vicar 'come across' them. I've suspected for a while that someone else had a key and I think it was him. The cabinet originally came from the vestry and obviously he had keys to all the offices. A couple of times I felt as though things had been disturbed and set a few traps. I don't know what to do, Ed. Do I come clean and let the cops have all of it, or do I go with my gut and say nothing?"

"I want to say it's a 'nutty' one, but that's only because I'm avoiding worse alternatives." Ed bit his bottom lip and gave the matter consideration. Then he looked at her strangely. "What traps?"

Jayden smirked. "I went through this period of feeling as though someone was coming in after I had left and reading my notes, especially those belonging to St Jude's congregation members. Things just seemed out of sequence when I went back for them and I know how I like to leave things for next time. Also, he would ask me how so-and-so was getting on and stuff like that. So I left a little surprise in a client's file one night recently and it seemed to stop after that."

"What surprise?" Ed's curiosity was so stirred that his forehead almost touched Jayden's as he leaned forward in anticipation.

"A mouse trap." Jayden sat back with a look of guilt mingled with satisfaction. Ed laughed outright.

"Oh my goodness woman! Remind me not to get on the wrong side of you!"

"The next day he had this massive bandage on one of his fingers. I didn't know where to look and there was blood on the trap. It was one of those really spiteful ones. I don't think he risked it again. I just made sure that he heard me tell Sal that I had a mouse problem and had hidden traps all over the office and he scooted off as fast as his shiny shoes could carry him!"

Ed had begun to snigger and it was cute. His nose wrinkled up and his forehead creased, making him appear more like a naughty schoolboy than a man of the cloth.

"What shall I do then?" Jayden asked him, peering closely at a long scar on his index finger. It was rough and jagged, shiny where the skin had struggled to mend and left that odd patina that a difficult healing leaves.

"Look, I've met Mrs McLean and I don't think she could have done it for all the reasons that you've said. For now, how about we just 'forget' about her notes and leave it at that? If it comes up later, I'll say that you consulted me and I told you to leave it."

"No," Jayden shook her head. "I don't want you getting the blame. I'll take the fall for it. It just didn't sit right making the decision alone. Rita would definitely have said I should hand it over, but...I'm not best pleased with her at the moment." Jayden's face took on a sour look that didn't suit her and Ed stroked his thumb across the back of her hand. She looked down at their entwined hands and felt sad. "We shouldn't be doing this," she said, uncoupling her fingers from his.

"Why?" he asked bluntly, refusing for a fraction of a second to let her go. "We're both consenting adults and I'm not asking you to go to bed with me. I'm just holding your hand. I find you..."

Jayden gave a determined tug and released her fingers, holding them up in front of Ed's face to make him stop. "Raff said..." she began, but it was his turn to interrupt. The mood had plummeted suddenly.

"You need to stop listening to everything my brother says. There are things you don't know. I need to talk to you about his marriage proposal. He's acting as though you've accepted and I..."

Jayden stood up suddenly. All trace of the amicable conversation was over. Ed sighed and followed her out of the cafe, hit by the bracing winter cold outside in the street. "Jayd wait!" He tugged on her good arm and tucked it into his again. He felt uncharacteristically powerless and his heart sought the camaraderie of just a few minutes before.

He was aware that he was struggling to control his feelings for this unusual woman. She was in his thoughts every minute of the day. There was a vulnerability underneath all the hardness and he was aware that the veneer she had sealed over herself was a lie. He wanted to be with her so badly and yet the obstacles seemed insurmountable. Too many things were stacked up against any possible relationship. There was indeed his 'marriage' as Raff had so aptly called it, then there was a twelve year age gap, not to mention that Ed's time at St Jude's was almost at an end. Then there was the issue of his brother's infatuation with her, not to mention the 'other thing' that Ed would need to explain at some point. He wandered along with his heart in his boots, praying silently that his Maker would help him out some.

Back at the office, the cops had searched Cam's room and there had already been a huge row as they declared their intention to take his filing cabinet away completely, leaving him unable to do his job. Finding it bolted to the floor, they moved on to Jayden's room with relish at her reappearance, having cursorily sifted through and made a terrible mess of Cam's filing system.

Jayden watched six men go through her office fairly thoroughly. Two of them sat with gloves on, going through her counselling notes while she watched them from the comfort of her office chair. In truth, she was waiting for a reaction from them. Just one snigger at the very genuine problems experienced by the people she worked with, would be enough for her to lose her temper.

The young blonde cop came and plonked himself down opposite her. He smiled, but she didn't return his efforts at pleasantry. "Well, we've managed to eliminate both you and Reverend Abbadeli from our inquiries," he stated, looking strangely hopeful.

"That's nice," Jayden replied, without taking her eyes off the grey haired policeman currently reading her notes from the session with Clara. "Have you read enough yet?" she called across to him spitefully, watching his neck go slightly red with embarrassment. "I don't see how the fifteen-year-old rape victim who came here this morning for the first time, is actually what you should be looking for!"

The policeman closed the file without looking across at her and placed it back in the cabinet in the wrong place. Jayden gritted her teeth and clenched her jaw until it hurt. Her eyes flashed as she stared at the policeman opposite her. "The people in those case files are genuinely broken people. It's not gossip column stuff that you can all laugh about in the police canteen! Some of them have had horrific experiences that have wrecked their lives and he just stands there reading it like some trashy magazine. I'm sure if you want real gory, your colleague's case file should have actual photographs of her injuries back at the station. I gather they were particularly unpleasant, being as she was so young and untried. Would you like me to ring your chief constable and ask for personal copies for you?"

All of the policemen seemed uncomfortable and embarrassed by her outburst. Some of it was making difficult reading, even for these seasoned officers.

"Then why don't you give us a clue, Miss Mitchell?" the detective asked, too nicely. Jayden felt trapped and knew that she couldn't just sit here watching them search the files of decent people with such detachment without exploding.

"Oh, hazelnut whirl *off!*" she said with real feeling and marched out of the room.

She sought solace in the body of the old church, slumping down in one of the pews near the back, behind one of the imposing stone pillars. They had been worn smooth by centuries of people pushing past them. Jayden leaned forward in her unforgiving seat and rested her warm forehead against its cool solidity. She closed her eyes and felt the pulse of the building, made up of the muffled clamour of the city outside; traffic, people moving around, phones ringing and voices rising and falling. Yet the church remained still and constant, an immovable force that would give an earthquake a run for its money. A bit like God really.

The pew moved as someone sat down gently next to her and Jayden opened her eyes and turned. She wasn't surprised to see Ed sitting close to her on the wooden seat. "Sorry about before," he whispered. "You and Raff, it's nothing to do with me."

He looked unbelievably sad and vulnerable; his dark brow furrowed and a lock of hair sticking out at the side where he had shoved his vicar's dress thingy on over his head. Jayden had this sudden overwhelming urge to look up it to see if he had kept his trousers on. Perhaps it was like the mystery with Scotsmen and their kilts. She still had no idea if they wore underpants beneath them or not. Ed's face broke into a tight smile, as though he had already guessed what she was thinking. The crow's feet reappeared at the outer corners of his eyes and he bit his bottom lip.

Jayden looked at him hard, desperate to feel that same contact with him that they had shared that night at her flat when he kissed her so sensuously on the mouth. She took a risk. Leaning forward so that her breasts were against his chest, she closed her eyes and kissed him, feeling the rising confusion in her chest as she felt the bristles on his skin against her cheeks and the smooth fullness of his lips. He kissed her eagerly back, his breath coming in a short hiss as he pulled her harder into him. Jayden had the fleeting thought that he had no perception of how much trust she was giving him, how much of her guard she was lowering just for him. She prayed that he wouldn't break her heart, whilst knowing inwardly that he was going to.

A wave of embarrassment penetrated the pure unadulterated lust that had filled Jayden's psyche and she pulled away with an anguished breath. But Ed wouldn't let her run away from him, wrapping his arm firmly around her shoulders and cuddling her strongly into his side. "God!" Jayden moaned softly in misery and felt Ed's soft kiss on her temple.

"Definitely," he answered, but Jayden didn't understand and couldn't face asking him what he meant. "They're pulling the vestry apart. Again," he sighed. "That's why I'm wandering around in here. Cam's gone home in a temper. I guess it's the same in your office?"

Jayden nodded her head, hearing the sound of her curly hair moving against the curate's cotton clothing. It sounded nice. "They haven't got a clue," she said nastily. "They're as thick as pig…praline."

Ed snorted and kissed her temple again, reaching his foot up to rest against the back of the pew in front. Jayden didn't know that he was allowed to do that. The church always seemed so sacrosanct and precious. She had seen little children on a Sunday get smacked bottoms for less. Jayden looked at Ed's shoes. They were nice shoes, square-toed and trendy. Quite designer Italian actually. Her eyes travelled to his socks, which were black and then she spied the hem of his black trousers poking out from underneath his dress. Myth busted. Scotsmen probably wore undies too then. It was a little disappointing.

Jayden's left arm began to ache with the constriction and she sat up slightly, shifting it so that it lay on Ed's stomach. Then she snuggled back down into him. He released his tight hold on her and rested his right arm along the back of the pew behind Jayden, his long fingers spooling through her curls absentmindedly. They were both relaxed and it felt so *right*.

"Where did the vicar go splat?" Jayden asked suddenly and it sounded so inappropriate and disrespectful in the holy hush of the church.

"Over there, next to the organ," Ed answered. "A lady came to do the flowers early and found him. There was blood everywhere."

"Are they still looking for the thing he was hit over the head with?" Jayden persisted, not sure why such details were important. Ed yawned.

"No, they found it. There was a hammer underneath the organ with his blood all over it. That's why they let us back into the church yesterday.

"Did you clean it up?" Jayden's face held sympathy and horror as she poked her face out to the side to look at him. Ed smiled and kissed her lightly on the lips again, pulling away when the tempting spark between them began to flare.

"No. The police forensic people did it. They made me come in afterwards and asked me to look and see if anything was different. That's when I noticed the chip in the flagstones by the organ. I dropped a thing of incense the day before and spent ages clearing it up, so I knew the floor quite well. The chip was new and led them to the hammer. It had wedged itself quite tightly underneath the organ, near the back - that's how come they missed it the first time. It must have gone under there with quite some force because it took off a lump of wood on its way in. The police think it fell from the balcony after it was used and somehow spun off under the organ, or was maybe kicked there afterwards. But they think it dropped, bounced on the stone a few times and skidded. Perhaps we'll never know."

Jayden was silent as her brain worked overtime. She realised that a nagging doubt had remained in her subconscious that perhaps Ed *had* killed the man, although the detective had implied that she and Ed had inadvertently alibied each other, despite her reluctance to mention seeing him. Why would Ed be pointing out clues to the cops if he had killed the vicar? Yet she had seen the two men arguing and then there was the issue of her front door key. The last thought sobered her up somewhat and she leaned forward in her seat, remembering the dark head and the fluro shirt disappearing up the High Street before dawn. "Where did you run this morning?" Jayden broached it, suddenly needing to know. Ed looked at her curiously.

"At the gym. I used Raff's car to get there. I had a seven o'clock meeting with the Dean up at the cathedral."

"So you didn't run past my place just after six?"

Ed shook his head. "No. I would have still been at the gym then. I hung around for Raff for a bit because he said he was going to run there, but he never showed up. I had a shower at the gym and got changed, dropped the car back and then walked over to the cathedral. Why? And why did you ask me if I had a nice run earlier? I would have noticed if you were at the gym."

The way he said that made Jayden's heart flutter like the wings of a baby bird. The thought that he had been looking out for her made her feel special, beautiful in some way. He looked so honest and trustworthy sitting there on the pew in his vicar's dress-surplice-cassock-thingy. *Mistrust* floated around above Jayden's head squawking at her that all men were liars, but she brushed him off easily for once, leaning in for another gentle kiss from the gorgeous man sitting next to her. She knew that she was truly smitten and that it was dangerous, but Jayden felt powerless to resist him as he kissed her back tenderly.

To her surprise he pulled away after what felt like very little time, cleared his throat and stood up. Her brow furrowed and she looked hurt, until he held out his hand to pull her up. "You're going to drive me mad," he whispered, running his thumb across her full lips. "I can't give in to temptation, no matter how much I want to. We're going to have to wait."

He moved as though to kiss her again and then corrected himself, keeping hold of her hand as they squeezed between the pews to the aisle. Then he let go and it felt like a slap to the head. Ed turned and saw the look on Jayden's face, turning back to speak to her and stroke her cheek. "No Jayd. Don't think bad thoughts about me, please? I'm falling in love with you, but there are things I need to sort out first. Wait for me?"

His question held a plea which Jayden responded to with a nod, drawing a smile from Ed's worried face. But the spectre of a wife hung suddenly over her and she felt unsavoury. She had counselled enough divorcees to know the trail of damage the process left behind it. And children. What if Ed had children? She had never asked. There seemed so much she didn't know about him and it piled up into an insurmountable mound of jagged rock.

Ed let go of her hand in the aisle, unaware of the route her brain was taking her. He stared up at the balcony above the organ and appeared to be considering the Reverend McLean's undignified fall. He placed his fingers over his mouth, splayed out to cover the bottom half of his face as he thought out loud. "So it wasn't you and it wasn't me. Cam and Sal had gone home. There was nobody here when I left, just him. So it had to have been someone who came back. Someone with a key, because I locked the front doors when I left and checked all the others. His wife couldn't have followed him up the stairs. I agree, she's far too crippled. The poor woman's feet face in opposite directions and her walking frame would be too wide for the doorway up there anyway." He turned to Jayden with a determined look on his face. "Who else is there, Jayd? Can you think of anyone else that he's upset recently? Anything?"

"Brian, he was mean to Brian," Jayden fumbled helplessly.

Ed shook his head. "A curate in a pub, wearing a full cassock is a pretty good alibi." He smiled wanly at her.

"You," Jayden said, surprising him fully. "I saw you arguing. I heard McLean say, '*How dare you?*' What was that over?"

"I've talked to the cops about that already," Ed said warningly. "I *will* tell you, but not right now. You didn't help your own case not corroborating that you saw me though, love."

"Right," Jayden replied and her tone was flat and disinterested, as though the rebuff had killed all sense of cooperation. "I should go," she said, faking urgency. "I was meant to stay in the room while they were searching. Goodness knows what kind of a mess they've made." She turned on her heel and was gone, her boots echoing over the stone floors and drowning out Ed's impassioned plea for her to stay.

Jayden got back to her office to find her filing cabinet on its back on the reception floor, nuzzling next to Cam's.

"We're done here," the blonde cop informed her. "If you could just sign to acknowledge that we're taking these two cabinets please?"

"Just get lost," Jayden retorted, inwardly astounded at her own rudeness. Lily McGowan giggled wickedly inside her, making her lips round with the smallest smirk. Left alone to grow up, Lily would have possessed all of her father's dry wit and her mother's forthright manner. Jayden snatched her coat from the closet where she had stowed it and grabbed her handbag from a hook behind the door.

The cops had been in the closet but clearly decided not to wrestle the huge fake tree down from the top shelf. It was heavy and took three strong congregation males to manhandle it each December. It was as though Christmas hadn't officially started until some poor sucker had got back pain. Stuffing it back in was usually worse than getting it out because gravity was definitely working against them. "Lock up when you leave. *Please.*" Jayden commented bitingly, glancing at her precious, confiscated office keys on the wooden desk and swished out of the building and into the afternoon. Poor Sal had been forced to cancel everyone's appointments and had gone home with stress. Hardly surprising.

At the end of the crazy paved walk, on the last turn before the church yard, Jayden literally ran into a tall elderly man. He caught her as she tumbled, accidentally yanking on her broken arm in his efforts to prevent her sprawling on the ground. She cried out in agony and was met with heartfelt apologies. "Cecil," she said, trying to keep the painful catch out of her voice as she fought the ache in her elbow. "How are you?"

"I wanted to see young Campion if I may," he said, removing his tweed cap and twisting it relentlessly in his hands. "I'm not really coping see, not with my Beryl gone. I thought he might be able to help me."

Jayden rested her good hand gently on the man's forearm. Poor Cecil. A memory came to her again, the faithful church organist, gaily and dutifully stroking the organ keys throughout the dreadful cancer that had begun in her lymph nodes and eaten at her body without relenting. Sporting a pretty pink headscarf, thoughtfully bought for her by the church ladies' group to cover her embarrassment at her bald head, Beryl had issued sweet music for the services even up until the week before she had gone to meet her Lord. There was little wonder that Cecil Macdonald was bereft, just a few short months on. He was like an odd shoe, lonesome and useless without its mate. The grief process was a three-year cycle and there were no shortcuts, despite man's attempts to manufacture many different cures.

"The police are all over the church, Cecil," Jayden

said gently, not sure if the man was even aware of what day it was, let alone that the vicar had plunged to his death over his favourite balcony. "I can get Cam to ring you tomorrow, or if you can't wait, the curate is in the church. Do you want me to come back with you and..."

"Nay," Cecil said dismissively. He was old school. A real Lincolnshire gentleman but his tone was uncharacteristically rough. "I don't want to talk to that idiot!"

Jayden was startled until she realised that he was probably referring to McLean's sidekick. Brian hadn't been seen around much since his superior's demise, but it was clear that his alibi had been thoroughly scrutinised. "Cecil," Jayden called to him as he turned away from her, "do you still have a church key?" She felt mean asking, as though she was driving home some kind of final rejection, but the man shook his head slowly and answered,

"Nay lass. Vicar came t'ospital and took it off our Beryl. Two days afore she died. It was the only visit he paid my poor lass. *Bastard!*" The broken man clamped his cap down hard over his head, yanking it until it touched his ears. He waved a disconsolate hand over his shoulder at her, not even giving her a chance to explain that Ed was better than the 'idiot.' She contemplated going back in and getting Ed to go after the poor man, but shied away from the feelings she got when she was near him. It felt overwhelming. He had said that he was falling in love with her...but...

Don't they always! Cynicism screeched at her from overhead. Her subconscious registered the half-truth as fact and with a shrug, Jayden set off home.

A nagging thought played on her mind all the way

up the High Street, not seeming to want to go away. Why on earth would Brian go to the pub in his full rig out and make a loud and raucous scene for himself. Unless he was deliberately looking for an alibi. The pub he favoured was literally down the street, about five hundred metres to the south. It was a big Irish bar with sawdust on the floor and regular fights. He would often spend his lunch hour there and stagger back more than a little worse for wear, sleeping the afternoon away on a pew. He had gotten worse lately. The Reverend McLean had taken enormous delight in waking him up sharply in all manner of unkind ways, including cups of tea poured over him from the balcony.

CHAPTER TWENTY-ONE

Jayden stopped dead in the middle of the street, not a great idea when the afternoon shopping rush was in full flood. A woman laden down with straining carrier bags tutted loudly as she circumnavigated Jayden's statuesque frame stopped rigidly in the walkway. "Get out t'bloody road!"

Jayden's calves were roughly banged with the contents of the bags, the hard corner of a cereal box and the clang of a tin on her ankle bone. Jayden hurried home, desperate to process her thoughts in peace.

Alas, it was not meant to be. Raff appeared as she was letting herself in, pushing his way in behind her and holding both his hands palm upwards in front of him by way of apology. He was smartly dressed in a suit with a shirt and tie and looked dazzlingly handsome. He kicked off his patent shoes and slouched up the stairs with his hands in his pockets, throwing himself onto the sofa before Jayden had managed to get her boots off and crest the stairs to the living room. She laid her handbag on the glass table and then went to stand over Raff, still with her outdoor coat on. Jayden held her hand out. "Key!" she said sharply and Raff visibly quailed.

"I just..." he began but Jayden raised her eyebrow and stared him down. Raff stood up and delved in his trouser pocket, where he retrieved the shiny silver key to Jayden's sanctuary.

"What are you playing at?" she demanded and he rubbed his hand across his face and looked pathetic.

"I thought if I came round early and...well, I thought that if I could prove to you that it would work - that we could be a couple, then..."

Jayden slipped her coat off and laid it over the back of the chair that she then slumped down in. "So explain to me how we went from a marriage of convenience to you trying to crawl into my bed at dawn! Have you any idea what that would have done to me? *Can you imagine how horrifying it would be to wake up and find a sweaty guy climbing into bed with you?*"

Jayden knew that she was wasting her time as a faintly hopeful look crossed Raff's face. It was a stupid question. He would probably enjoy it. "It's not going to happen, Raff. You're my friend - well, at least you were until you started trying to make it into something else. Just come clean with your family and have done with it, or live a life of celibacy and do something useful."

"What like my perfect brother?" Raff asked spitefully. "The perfect son. I can never match up to him."

"You aren't expected to," Jayden counselled him, hearing the previously hidden cry of his heart. "He loves you as you are. The only person making it into a competition is you."

Raff shook his head. "Na, you don't get it. I saw my folks last week and all they could talk about was grandchildren. They kept asking about you and it kind of put this idea in my head. I felt so guilty. They would make amazing grandparents. It's not their fault they ended up with a monk and a poofter."

"Raff!" Jayden felt exhausted all of a sudden. His

deprecation of himself was pitiful, but part of her warned that in her tired state, she could be easily manipulated by someone as skilful as the man in front of her. It must have taken great talent to play act for as long as Raff had. She didn't want to be part of the continuance of a thirty-year deception. The irony was that she might have considered it seriously only a matter of months ago but now, her senses had tasted love and weren't prepared to settle for anything less.

"So is it a definite *no* then?" Raff asked, always a man renowned for trying.

Jayden shook her head and smiled at him. "No, Raff. I can't marry you. We both deserve better than some sham marriage and children who don't know which way is up. We probably both crave what our parents had and nothing less will satisfy either of us. One or both of us will end up finding our soul mate and detonate the whole thing. It would be devastating in the end."

Raff leaned his forearms on his thighs and sank forwards, not so much in disappointment but resignation. Jayden felt sorry for him but couldn't forget his attempts to seduce her against her will. Raff had no idea what she had been through, but even so, it had been a stupid thing to do to a friendship built on shaky trust. "Don't suppose you fancy going to the pub?" Jayden asked him with a smile.

"Which one?" Raff perked up, naming a few of the higher end bars at the top of town. He was decidedly less keen when she mentioned the Irish pub south of the church. "Why would you want to go there?" he asked in amazement.

"Because I do and because you owe me after this morning's little..."

"I don't think it's an Irish pub anymore. You won't like it."

"Fine!" Jayden said crossly, instantly withdrawing her proffered olive branch.

"Ok, ok," Raff conceded. "But if I get seduced or beaten up, it will be all your fault!"

O'Shea's was different to how Jayden remembered it. She walked into town with Raff, relieved that their former, easy companionship had been restored. Jayden had hidden her cast underneath a flowing top and long coat and walked arm in arm with her friend. Raff stayed dressed in his suit; the expensive blue striped shirt opened at the top. He had left his tie on Jayden's dining table. "Oh, the *Shea's* has fallen off!" she exclaimed in surprise as they turned to face the front doors. "It's just *O's* now. How funny."

Raff shook his head, humouring her and smirked slightly. Inside, it had clearly undergone a massive refurbishment. The comfortable green velveteen booths had been replaced by high tables and bar stools. Gone was the sawdust which had covered the wooden floors, piled high in the corners. It had gotten everywhere, in shoes, inside clothing and into drinks. But it had added a rustic effect and been student friendly and homely in a strange kind of way. It had also mopped up the beer spills from drunken collisions and probably other more distasteful bodily substances.

Jayden stopped dead in the entrance, causing Raff to run into the back of her. She turned to him with a look of confusion as she took in the dark blue walls and designer wallpaper over the bar area. He rolled his eyes and dug his fingers into her back, to move her on as a large and impatient group of people bulged behind him looking for the reason for the bottleneck. "I wanted a *Dancing Leprechaun*," she pouted crossly and Raff laughed openly at her.

"I'd just settle for a Fit Irishman," he chortled, making up his own drink on the spot.

At the bar, Jayden peered at the drinks dangling temptingly from optics behind the barman. "A merlot please," she conceded and the young blonde man leaped to do her bidding, skilfully tossing a glass one-handed and holding it under the red wine optic with a flourish. Raff smiled and nudged her with his elbow playfully.

"I did try to tell you," he said but Jayden looked away, tempted to tell him that he hadn't tried hard enough.

Some of the high tables had bar stools and some didn't, encouraging drinkers to stand around their rounded surface and chat. Jayden pulled a face and hauled herself up onto a high seat. Raff plonked his vodka down on the table and pulled up a stool. "I used to love this pub," Jayden sulked. "My psychology tutor group used to meet in here once a week to go over our essays and lecture notes. It was always lively and sometimes they had loud music."

"Sounds yum," Raff breathed sarcastically and Jayden pouted more. "Come on," he said kindly, reaching out and holding her hand, "we're here now. Let's just enjoy our drinks and leave. Why did you want to come here anyway?"

Jayden leaned in close and conspiratorially. "I heard that the Reverend McLean's curate drinks here most days and I have this horrid feeling that he knows more about the vicar's murder than he's making out."

Raff shook his head. "May the good Lord save us all from female amateur sleuths!"

"Don't be so rude. It was just a hunch. Anyway, he doesn't seem to be here so it doesn't matter."

"He wouldn't be in here at all. He's a clergyman for goodness sake. He *shouldn't* be in here."

"Christians are allowed to drink, silly. They just aren't allowed to get drunk." Feeling a little foolish, Jayden tried to change the subject as they sipped their drinks and listened to the melodic music piping out of the speaker above their head. The delicious scent of hot chips wafted out from a table nearby where a little knot of men shared bar snacks. Jayden put her hand to her stomach as she felt its agonised growl.

Raff had paid for the drinks, so Jayden ordered the chips and handed over her card. A girl at the end of the bar smiled and waved to her and Jayden smiled back. Perhaps it wasn't such a bad place after all. People certainly seemed friendly. "They've got a Queen tribute band on Saturday," Jayden said conversationally, clambering back up onto the tall stool.

"How appropriate," Raff responded, sarcasm dripping from the sentence.

"What's Ed's wife like?" Jayden pretended that she was attempting to change the subject but knew that really, she was just torturing herself.

"Horrid. And she hates me!" he retorted.

"Oh," Jayden couldn't imagine Ed married to someone like that. "Is he happy with her?"

"Blissfully," Raff snapped. "Please can we talk about something else?"

Jayden was perplexed. "Yes, ok, but...why would she hate you?"

Raff heaved an exaggerated sigh and answered through gritted teeth. "Because I'm gay, that's why!"

Jayden reacted as though she had been slapped. So somehow, Ed's wife knew that his brother was gay, but Ed didn't. It didn't make sense, but Raff's face told her to leave the subject well alone for now. Jayden's eye was caught by a sudden movement over near the toilets that lay at the rear of the pub. A dark shape staggered down the narrow passageway and lurched out into the bar.

The curate wore his black clothes, complete with dog-collar and he reeled from side to side, clearly inebriated. He weaved with difficulty through the knots of people, unsteady and precarious on his comfortable rubbery shoes. His puffy, flaccid face looked pale and sick and his eyes were unfocussed. He banged into Raff on the way past and then noticed Jayden, looking curiously at him as he swayed on his legs. Raff moved away, keen not to be part of any unnecessary trouble, but Brian pointed directly at Jayden and almost poked her companion in the eye. "Little Miss Perfect," he drawled nastily. Then he said a string of swearwords that almost turned the air blue. "He thought you were bloody perfect, you prissy little bitch. God, if only he knew what you really are. I wish I could have told him. You're nothing but a fraud!"

Jayden's swallow stopped dead in her throat and the drink slid uncomfortably down into her gullet. *How could this man know anything about her? How could he know what she was?* Her brain began to work overtime. Nick must have gone to the church and talked to the curate about her. He would have told him her real name, what had happened - everything. It was too awful to contemplate. A sane little voice in her head repeatedly asked her what Nick could hope to gain from doing that, but Jayden didn't want to listen to reason and dismissed it easily. As the bouncers made their way over to the slavering Brian and bodily took him outside with a minimum of fuss, Jayden skulled her drink and asked if they could leave.

"Don't be worrying about him!" Raff said in annoyance. "Look, our chips are here now."

Jayden suddenly wasn't hungry. The few chips that she managed to get down seemed to stick at every piece of cartilage in her gullet, before landing like a brick in her stomach. The girl over at the bar kept on staring at her and all feelings of safety and joviality had disappeared by the time Raff had wiped the last chip around the tomato sauce smudge in the bottom of the bowl. Pushing her stool back impatiently, Jayden felt it connect with something behind her and turned sharply.

A congregation member from St Jude's rubbed at his thigh where the stool edge had belted him.

"Oh, sorry Barney," Jayden apologised. "These are so high and hard to manage."

The man she had accidentally assaulted was tall and extremely handsome. He was blonde in a surf-bum kind of way and had the lithe body of one who kept himself extremely fit. Usually he was confident and self-assured but his manner now was almost shifty and furtive. He eyed Jayden nervously, as though she had unlimited power to destroy his world. His face had a slight dusting of blonde-end-of-the-day-stubble that still couldn't cover the embarrassed flush which lit up his tanned skin. Instantly Jayden took responsibility for his reaction to her, fearing that she had offended him in some way and felt the strong fingers of *Guilt* on her shoulder. "I'm so sorry," she said again, pushing her dark locks away from her pretty face discomfited, huge green eyes misting over with concern.

Barney attempted to brush it off lightly, claiming that he was absolutely fine. Raff remained seated, having grown fond of the bar and not ready to leave. He didn't understand Jayden's hurry. "Barney," the blonde man said, holding out his hand to Raff.

Raff smiled nicely and shook hands with the other man, appraising him covertly and sizing up the well-toned body, clear skin, striking hazel eyes and silky, overlong hair.

"This is my friend, Raff," Jayden said, seeing her quick escape disappearing. Barney seemed happy to disconnect from the group of males he was standing with, retrieving his pint of lager from their table and pulling up a stool to sit with Raff. Jayden gave up and returned to the bar, getting three fresh drinks and struggling to carry them back to the table. She couldn't do it and had to leave Raff's on the bar and return for it separately.

"Hi," the girl from the bar said, sounding confident. "I'm Lorna."

"Jayden," the dark haired beauty replied, feeling suddenly self-conscious.

"I haven't seen you here before."

"No," Jayden felt flustered. "I came to see my curate, but he's a bit worse for wear and I think he's left now."

"Oh yeah, Reverend Brian, he comes in here a lot."

Deciding that the conversation could be quite useful, Jayden hung around for a moment, trying to show willing by taking a sip of Raff's horrid drink. "Yes I came looking for him last week. He had all his robes on and didn't want to talk."

"I remember that!" Lorna giggled, tossing her red straightened hair like a model. She was very beautiful. "That was the night he got really wrecked and cut his face."

"Cut his face?" Jayden interrupted, wracking her brain. "I don't remember seeing him with a cut on his face."

"Well, he did have," the girl replied, suspicion creeping into her voice. "Are you a cop?"

Jayden snorted and laughed. She obviously wasn't very good at this sleuthing lark. "No way! He owes me some money actually." It was the first thing that came into her head.

"How much?" Lorna persisted. Jayden pondered an amount. It was a surprisingly difficult question. It had to be enough to make her go after him for it, but not too much to be unrealistic.

"Four hundred and one pounds," she said conspiratorially, adding, "and fifty pence." For some reason, it was the shameful exactitude of the lie that clinched it and made her sound convincing.

"Crikey, I'd be after him for that as well." Lorna sipped a gin and tonic and Jayden took another unbearable swig of the vodka. *Yuk*. A glance over at Raff found him deep in conversation with Barney. She didn't think he had even missed her. To her annoyance, she saw him take a deep swallow of her lovely red wine. She pulled a face.

"I wonder how he cut his face," Jayden mused out loud. She had seen him around the place repeatedly since the murder; sallow-faced and dour, but not displaying anything likely to have bled overly much.

"He did it outside," Lorna said factually. "He was in the bogs for ages throwing up and then he went out the front. He was gone for a while and came in with blood on his cheek. Then he slumped down in his usual seat over there," she indicated a comfy sofa next to a fake wood burner that was throwing out orange light like an inferno. Pointing with her index finger, Lorna kept her glass in her hand. "He started shouting around midnight and the bouncers threw him out. End of." Lorna smiled at Jayden, a hint of something unreadable in her face. "I haven't seen you in here before. Have you just come out?"

Jayden nodded, trying not to grimace at the taste of the vodka, which now wouldn't leave her palate.

"It's hard isn't it?" Lorna scooted her stool over to where Jayden was stood and reached out for a lock of Jayden's dark hair, shifting it tenderly behind the other woman's ear. Jayden was rooted to the spot, feeling suddenly vulnerable.

"I came out with my friend," Jayden said in a small voice, aware that she hadn't a clue what was going on, just that something was.

"Oh, is he gay too?" Lorna looked over at Raff with real interest. "I'm bi as well. It's nice to have people who know how you feel. Is he a *really* good friend?"

Jayden felt unexpectedly very hot all over. She sensed the influx of sweat drip unpleasantly down from the small of her back into her knickers. Was there actually any point trying to explain that she thought Lorna meant 'come out' as in 'come out to the pub' or would it make her look an idiot? Summoning all her counselling resolve and personal pride, she drew herself up to her full height and smiled benevolently down on Lorna. "I should get back," she said sweetly. "It's been lovely to talk."

Waving over her shoulder and trying not to trip over, Jayden scurried over to the table, giving Raff eye signals of alarm that he completely ignored. "I think I might get a taxi home," she said after another half an hour and a round of drinks, which she made Raff fetch. She had switched to lemonade.

"That's ok," he said nicely. "I'll walk you home and then get off. I've got an early shift tomorrow."

At the use of the words 'get off' Jayden flinched at the unintended connotation that flooded unbidden into her mind and shuddered visibly. She climbed down off her stool, avoiding Lorna's gaze from her perch at the bar and was surprised when Barney leaned in and kissed her on the cheek. "Lovely to see you, Jayden."

He looked so fondly at her that she knew she had missed something major. She was completely out of her depth, as though in her counselling room she could cope with anything but out in the real world, surprises had the power to throw her hideously off course. Jayden smiled back up into his sincere face and hoped that she was giving off all the right signals. It wasn't difficult. Barney was a genuinely lovely guy and hung with the twenty-somethings who lurked at the back of the church on a Sunday morning, listening to the ramblings of the Reverend McLean. Only now, it wouldn't be his ramblings they sat and texted or worried through, but Eds...

With an appeal for help at Raff's happy face, Jayden bid Barney goodbye and headed for the ornate double doors, which still bore the betrayed monogram of O'Shea's Bar, frosted onto the glass. Reluctantly, Raff followed her outside into the bitter cold January air. They had just begun walking when he stopped dead, a horrified look on his face. "Damn, I left my phone on the table. I won't be a sec."

With that, he was gone, leaving Jayden stood alone in the darkened High Street. A few cars swooped by, hurrying to their destinations, headlights glinting and sparkling off the wet pavement. Jayden supported her cast in her right hand after pulling her coat tightly around her torso. It was too hard to pop the buttons through the holes in the dark one-handed, so she didn't even bother.

Raff was more than just a second and Jayden began to wonder if she should go back in and wait for him inside the doorway. Shifting herself back towards the wall, she didn't see the dark shape on the ground behind her and almost fell, righting herself just in time as she saw the grey pavement coming up to meet her. The shape grunted as Jayden leapt away, untangling its dark mass to reveal two chunky legs and a stumpy body.

The curate rose up from the ground, using the walls to climb up. He seemed confused and befuddled and Jayden felt momentarily sorry for him. He had been sick on the street and some of it ran down his black shirt in a creamy rivulet which stank of second-hand alcohol. He focussed his eyes, seeing the dark hair and pale face staring at him and reacted before Jayden could move away. His clumsy hand shot out without warning and he gripped the lapels of Jayden's warm winter coat, hauling her towards him. She could feel the heat of his breath and scent the vomit as his vaporous fumes licked her face. She made the mistake of thinking initially that he wanted her to help him up, until he pushed his visage into hers and threatened her with a voice that hissed through his teeth like a snake. "So, she's no better than the rest of us, is she?"

Jayden's brain worked overtime, trying to figure out who they were meant to be talking about, realising suddenly with a jolt that he was pointing his other wavering hand at her. "Little Miss Fantastic," he continued with a sneer. "He thought you were marvellous." Brian staggered momentarily, still gripping Jayden's coat and almost pulling her down with him. He made his voice sound high and screechy, alarming in the quiet street as he did an impression of the Reverend McLean. *"She's so amazing that girl. She can talk to all the weirdoes and misfits in our congregation. Just send them all to her and she'll train them out of it…"*

Saliva cascaded down his chin and spotted on the pavement as he lolled slightly on his unsteady feet but still didn't release her. In desperation, Jayden let go of her cast, using her right hand to try and pry his fingers off her coat but he was locked on, as much to keep himself upright as to detain the frightened female. He leaned towards her precariously and Jayden thought that she might vomit herself. She fought to stop Brian's florid face morphing into Wes', working overtime to stay in the present moment and prevent herself being dragged backwards, to another time, another place, a whole other life.

"Everyone loves you and all the time; you're as much of a fake as I am," Brian slavered. "Geez, I wish that mean old bastard was here to see it. Mind you, I could just tell the other one couldn't I? Tell the bishop everything I know about the saintly counsellor. Maybe I will. Maybe I won't. But you'll be out on your ear, lady. I'm gonna make sure..."

Brian lurched again, dragging Jayden to the left and causing her cast to jab into her side wickedly. The subsequent pain in her elbow joint produced the necessary impetus to galvanise her into changing her circumstances. With a well-remembered self-defence move, she turned her right-hand palm facing inwards, making the outer edge of it like a blade and chopped downwards against the cleric's wrist joint. It wasn't hard enough, nor was it completely in the right place and sent a jarring pain up her hand and into her shoulder, but it was enough to make him let go.

It wasn't completely necessary to do anything else as the man wobbled and his torso sank lower, folding over his legs like an envelope flap, but Jayden's previous inactivity and sudden late start had put the self-defence process into motion. Using her right elbow, she turned slightly and jabbed it into the priest's flaccid face, hearing the crack of bone on bone as it connected. He went down like a sack of potatoes falling over on itself, hitting the floor with a jolt. His head lay dangerously near Jayden's foot and she lifted it, fully intending to stomp down on the skull beneath. He had ceased to be the idiotic, ungodly, lazy waste of space which the congregation barely tolerated, talking about him behind their hands. He had morphed into Wes fully, the gimlet eyes ravishing Lily's innocent body even while his scarred hands ripped her skirt and tore her underwear away from her, without an ounce of regard for the teenager's future. She felt the searing, humiliating sensations as keenly as if it had happened only yesterday and could taste powerlessness on her tongue. Jayden saw the cleric's bald pate, its paleness reflecting the street lights and imagined the release that crushing it into the concrete would give her. It would be over. Finally. Her foot closed on the pale shape of Brian's head.

"Jayden! No! What the hell are you doing?" Raff's voice penetrated her focussed brain with difficulty, sounding blurred and distorted through the hazy mist of her rage. He seized her shoulders in his hands as *Murder* flitted overhead. Jayden placed her foot carefully on the concrete, noting the satisfying click that her boot heel made on the flagstone.

"He grabbed me," she said, bile dripping off the end of her sentence as she pushed Raff's restraining hand away from her bad arm. It ached. Her whole body ached each muscle, nerve and sinew reacting to the surge of adrenaline in her blood.

"He what?" Raff's voice went up at the end into a shriek that made Jayden's ears feel sensitive and he stepped back towards the man prone on the ground. He was alive still, grunting and moving around on the concrete on his face. One of the bouncers appeared from the front doorway, seeing Raff holding onto Jayden's wrist and the man on the ground.

"Not you again!" he said with disgust, hauling the curate up by his arm. Another round face had appeared on the steps, looking disembodied in its black suit in the darkness. The first bouncer looked back towards him and commanded, "Get this dickhead a taxi will you. Not Collin's or Yellow Cabs, they won't take him anymore. Try that other one. And hurry up. I'm not bringing him back inside. Otherwise, we won't get him out again. Someone needs to do something about this guy!"

Raff put pressure on Jayden's left arm above the cast, causing her to wince and move away from the scene. Then he gripped it hard and practically frog-marched her up the High Street. "Jayden..." he began but she reacted, pushing his hand off her arm and turning to face him.

"You left me!" she shouted at him, the rage still bubbling under the surface, desperately seeking any crack or fissure from which to escape. "How could you?" Her eyes were dry, not a single tear visible as she stared coldly at him.

"I was...I just...I was only a second..." he held out his hands, palm upwards in supplication and it was then that Jayden saw the guilt in his eyes.

"You weren't getting your phone were you?" Betrayal lit up her face like a mask, appearing gold and yellowed in the headlights of the passing cars. Raff looked away.

"Let's go home," he said.

But Jayden backed away from him, feeling the edge of the kerb beneath the balls of her feet, her heels already out over the gutter. It felt precarious and dangerous as though she was drunk. Only she wasn't. *What am I?*

A strange and unfamiliar power coursed through her veins as she faced down the disloyal friend. It all fell into place with horrible clarity. "What were you doing?" Her teeth were gritted so tightly together that she could barely open them to speak. Raff bit his lip and struggled to answer her.

"I was getting someone's phone number," he replied shamefaced. Then he took a step towards her. Big mistake.

"You left me outside in the dark, alone, to be

grabbed by a drunk so that you could get someone's number?"

Raff blanched at the cold, hard facts. "I'm sorry," he whispered. "It only seemed like a few seconds."

Jayden levered herself up onto the balls of her feet and set off marching towards him at a cracking pace. The neat right hook that Raff had spent hours teaching her in the gym landed precisely where it was supposed to, knocking him off balance with the unexpectedness of it. Jayden felt her mother's eternity ring sink into the skin on the bridge of his nose as his mouth opened wide with shock. He staggered backwards like a boxer but didn't fall, putting both hands up to his bleeding nose as his eyes began to water furiously. "Geez!" he exclaimed, leaning forwards to let the blood flow onto the ground and not onto his expensive imported suit jacket.

When he looked up, Jayden had gone, blending into the dark street as shadow and blurred snapshots. Raff attempted to catch up, but the blood flowed more willingly with each step and drove him back to his bent position over the pavement. By the time he had made his way up to the front door of her flat she was inside. Light from the second-floor window evidenced her safe arrival and Raff didn't have the courage to knock, knowing that she would ignore him anyway.

With incredibly sad footsteps he made his way home, breathing through his mouth all the way up Steep Hill, a journey encumbered by his hand wedged underneath his nose. When he finally knocked on the front door of his own home, grateful for the capable presence of Ed, his jacket was spattered and ruined and his face a mess. Ed was in his pyjama bottoms and for once, Raff allowed him to be his big brother, taking care of his wounds and listening to him, long into the night.

CHAPTER TWENTY-TWO

"Can I talk to you for a minute?" Ed's voice was calm and rational, catching Jayden as she turned to hang her coat in the closet. The view from her window was of the wall of the building next door and Jayden stared woodenly at it for a prolonged moment, before turning and holding her hand out towards the leather chairs in the seating area.

"I *would* quite like to talk to you," she said slowly, sounding guarded and closed. Ed paused, waiting politely. "I quit," Jayden said with a tight little smile. "I realise that somehow the curate found out about my past and threatened to tell everyone. I don't really need people's sympathy and questions so I quit. I can leave today."

Ed looked at her oddly. "Can you just run that by me again?" he asked, sounding a little pleading.

Jayden huffed slightly, as though speaking to someone of low intelligence and to whom she was trying to explain how to feed toilet roll onto a holder. "Has Brian been to see you?"

Ed winced at the frost in her voice. "Yes."

"Good then," she replied, standing up and going back over to the closet where she struggled to disentangle her coat from the hanger. "Then there's no more to be said."

"Well there is actually," Ed replied, standing up and moving towards her. His height was intimidating as he stared down at her. "Because he gave me this weird story about you being gay and then he quit."

Jayden's mouth shot open in surprise, her eyes round and startled. "Gay? Me?"

It was like being locked in a surreal episode of a soap opera. Realising that her arm was aching, Jayden gave up the battle with her coat and just stood there.

"He also said you assaulted him, which my brother corroborated last night, although in his version the curate grabbed you first. After which, you assaulted my brother. So, if you wouldn't mind just running the whole story by me from the beginning, I would be really grateful."

Jayden gaped like a fish. An ugly flapping fish; but didn't move. Her brain ticked through the previous evening, trying to work out if she had been on the same night out as Raff and the cleric, or if she had actually been in some alternate universe unbeknown to her waking self.

"Sit!" Ed ordered her authoritatively, snapping her out of her reverie. She walked shakily over to the chair adjacent to his and plonked herself into the leather. Ed watched her carefully. Leaning in, he took her right fingers gently in his large hand and rubbed the cold out of them, looking up into her eyes fondly. "Talk to me Jayd," he said softly. "What on earth is going on?"

"I'm not gay!" she blurted out, as though the whole idea was ludicrous. "That's not what he was going to tell you at all. He was going to tell you my real name and what happened to me. I don't know how he found out...maybe Nick came here and told him...he's going to tell the bishop. I don't want everyone to know. I need to just leave!"

Ed pulled his chair round to face Jayden's without

letting go of her twisting fingers. Their knees were almost touching as he leaned in towards her. She could feel his warm breath on her nose and mouth, the scent of toothpaste seeming so fresh after the curate's vomit-breath. Ed had cut himself shaving, a tell-tale speck of blood dotting his jawbone and Jayden had the overwhelming urge to launch herself into his chest, melt away inside his body and stay there forever, completely safe. She reached her hand up and touched his shirt front, resting her palm against his muscular chest, closing her eyes and grounding herself against his steady heartbeat. He moved his hand over hers and stroked her fingers again, a rhythmic, sensual touch that was hypnotic and helped her to believe that everything would be all right. "He got the wrong end of the stick. He assumed that because you were in a gay bar that you were gay."

"Gay bar." The pennies dropped into the slot of the arcade game with amazing clarity, the girl at the bar, Barney's surprise at meeting her there, Raff's ease in the place and Lorna's comment about Brian being there. She had said that he 'shouldn't' be there. The curate was gay.

"He killed Reverend McLean," Jayden said with surety. "He left the pub and went back to church. When he returned he had blood on him."

Ed nodded. "I know. The police are with him now. It seems that Reverend McLean was somewhat homophobic and they had a very unpleasant conversation in which McLean told him that he would be finished as a curate. Brian went away, got drunk and came back to talk to him. It all got out of hand. He's told me everything."

"But he was going to tell the bishop about me. He won't approve of someone counselling when they clearly haven't dealt with their own issues, so it doesn't matter what *you* think, because you're leaving anyway."

"We can deal with that," Ed said patiently. "But I need to talk to you about something else. Ironically, your brother Nick *has* been here."

Jayden's body reacted as though it had been attached to a live electric wire, jerking suddenly in her seat. Ed put his other hand reassuringly on her knee and refused to let her claim her right hand back from his chest. "It's ok," he soothed, "he came in a few days ago, just to sit for a while and we got talking. It took me a while to realise that it was you whom he was speaking about, but I figured it out quite by chance when he said that he had left a bunch of lilies at his sister's door." Ed kept the stroking motion going on Jayden's stiff fingers. "He would like to see you, before he goes away. He came in again yesterday and we agreed that I would approach you about it. But your decision is final, Jayd. Whatever you want, I promise I will do. If you want to see him, I can be there with you, or get your supervisor, whatever you want. And if you don't want to see him, that's fine, I will tell him so."

Jayden took a huge gulp of air and accidentally swallowed it, feeling her gullet constrict in pain and the gurgling begin at the top of her stomach. She felt sick. "Did he tell you...everything?" she asked, getting eye contact with the dark man in front of her. *Shame* and *Disgust* had not had access to Jayden's heart for a good few years but they floated near her face now, seeking to colour her pretty complexion and find a crack back into her psyche.

"He did," Ed admitted quietly, his blue eyes like pools of pain, "and it doesn't change the way I feel about you at all. I'm sorry it happened, but I'm not able to stop myself loving you, even if I wanted to, which I don't."

"Oh." His reply had been unexpected and Jayden had only been ready for rejection and humiliation. With a screech of despair, *Shame* and *Disgust* clung to each other near the ceiling. "He's been following me," she said, her voice flat and toneless.

"He's been waiting for you to talk to him," Ed said, sounding confused. "He pushed a letter through your letterbox a while ago asking to meet you. He said he would wait by the Stone Bow each night around five o'clock in case you decided to see him. The flowers were for your birthday."

Jayden smiled wanly. "Lily's birthday." She no longer celebrated it. "I didn't get any letter."

"Ok, it's irrelevant now. The thing is, Nick leaves in two days and is unlikely to come back to England. If you want to see him, I'm happy to facilitate it, but unfortunately, there isn't much time."

"Leaving?" Jayden felt stupid.

"It was all in the letter," Ed said gently. "Look," he made a decision. "There are other things that I need to talk to you about, but for now, just have a think about everything and let me know. Most of the counselling clients have cancelled this week, with everything that's gone on, so you have some time. Maybe talk it over with Cam or whoever you want." Ed stood up and flexed his fingers. Jayden's hand fell into her lap. "Sal say's you've just got Clara to see today and then that's it." Ed leaned down towards her, feeling pity well up in his chest and striking it away. It wasn't what she needed from him, nor was it what she deserved. "I love you," he said softly, seeing the tiny light that went on in her green eyes as she looked up at him. "Please don't forget that." He kissed her lightly on her upturned lips and then left the room, going into the now empty vestry to intercede for her with his God.

CHAPTER TWENTY-THREE

"I almost didn't come," Clara stated, the smallest hint of rebellion in her voice.

Me neither, the voice in Jayden's head intoned quietly. "Why did you?" she asked instead, feeling hideously ill-equipped for this session. Clara pouted slightly.

"It helped me before. I did the homework, but I could only think of five things that the man didn't take away from me. Not ten, just five."

"Five's good," Jayden said, trying to sound more positive than she currently felt.

"What would your ten be?" Clara asked searchingly. "Could you think of ten things?"

Jayden looked at her aghast. Nobody had asked her. She thought hurriedly for something to say, seeing the expectation on Clara's pretty blonde face. Her brown eyes glared out challengingly at Jayden, making her feel inadequate. Jayden shook her head. "I don't know."

Clara was displeased. "Well, you have to know. You're the counsellor. Ok then, what would you say my other five things were?"

Jayden held her hand out for a piece of paper in Clara's hand, but the girl refused to part with it. "No, you have to guess," she replied in an annoying sing-song voice, as though it was a harmless child's game. Jayden wasn't in control of this session and began to feel fearful. Her mind was elsewhere and she knew that she should call a halt to it. "Are your parents outside again?"

"No. What are my five things?"

Jayden gulped. Into her head popped the things that she had lost, the things that Clara still had. "You have your mother. You have your father. You have their love, unconditional acceptance and support. You have your home. You have your name."

Jayden looked down at her clipboard and the empty paper on it. Her pen was still in her hand, but nothing was coming out of it.

"Are those the things you lost?" Clara whispered.

Jayden nodded and a big fat tear ran from her right eye and plopped onto the paper. It was so bulbous that it exploded on impact and went through the top sheaf of pages. Clara was silent, contemplating the woman in front of her. She was so stiff and straight-backed, her dark hair under as much control as it was possible for rioting curls to be contained and her green eyes looked empty. "You lost more than me," Clara sighed. "Much more."

Jayden's head gave the smallest imperceptible nod. "I lost my brother too."

Never engage in a pity party; rule 101 of counselling. It was almost never helpful. To Jayden's surprise, Clara came over and sat on the arm of the leather chair. She put her slender arm gently around Jayden's shoulders. There was more to her than there had been a few days ago. Clara had finally started eating again. "I still have my mum and dad," she said. "And much as I want to punch his lights out half the time, I still have my little brother, the git. I guess that I'm still *me* too, deep down. I've always liked my name, *Clara*. It feels kind of sunny and yellow and I can't imagine changing it. So with my five, that's ten things. You're right. He didn't take everything, I only thought he did." Clara stood up and looked down at her counsellor. "Thanks, Jayden," she said generously. "I feel heaps better now."

With that, she turned and walked out of the room, her lightness of step marking the return of the fifteen-year-old girl who had not yet been violated. Deep inside Jayden, Lily McGowan stirred and sat up. In a crystal clear voice she brushed the dark tangle of hair out of her eyes and demanded, "*It's time.*"

CHAPTER TWENTY-FOUR

Despite wanting to comfort Jayden, Ed deliberately didn't touch her. She was unpredictable and shrouded in a pain that made her utterly unreachable. She was prickly like a hedgehog and he knew that no matter which way he tried to smooth her, he would end up with cut and bleeding fingers. He prayed for her and ached, as though his own heart-scars were being torn open with dirty hands. But there was nothing he could do.

A gentle knock on the vestry door heralded a tall man, broad-framed but slightly stooped. He was muscular rather than fat and his hair had receded to the point where it was cropped closely to his head. Nick McGowan did not look his twenty-nine years, but had aged far beyond that, resembling a man who had surely walked the earth for forty or more.

Jayden stood as he entered, not wanting to be compromised by being seated. She was stunned by her brother's resemblance to her father. Dan's green eyes and strong, square jaw faced her and it caused her to take a sharp intake of breath. Ed watched her carefully. They had agreed that if she were comfortable, he would wait outside in the stone hallway, within earshot if she needed him. Ed looked at her for some clue as to what she wanted, seeing immediately that she didn't yet know. He pulled open a cupboard in the wall, exposing a kettle, tea pot and some china cups. A small fridge nestled on the floor at knee level and he reached down into it for milk.

The room was utterly silent and Ed kept his back turned, not wanting to appear ghoulish or curious. He had clearly made Nick a drink before as he didn't ask him what he wanted, just produced a dark coloured tea. He handed Jayden coffee and she sipped at the too hot liquid, startled to taste the slight kick of alcohol.

Looking up in confusion, she caught the wink from Ed's stunning blue right eye. It was so momentary that it was only half there, but Jayden caught the sentiments; encouragement and love in the simple act of adding a tot of whiskey to her drink. She shook her head and let the tiniest smile crawl across her pretty lips in acknowledgement of the curate's lack of faith. Ed saw and felt relieved. He knew that his was a God of the impossible, but he was wise enough to know that Jayden wasn't so sure at the moment. "I'll just be outside," Ed said, nodding kindly at Nick and running his hand lightly across Jayden's shoulder. Inwardly she panicked, not wanting him to leave but unable to make him stay without causing a scene. Something told her that if she raised her voice or began a commotion, it would all be over, ruined. She stayed seated and peered out from under her eyelashes at her long-lost brother.

"Ed said that you didn't get my letter," Nick stated and Jayden nodded and looked up to meet his eyes. It surprised her that *Fear* seemed to have no control over her and that it was easier than she had expected it to be. "Would you like me to tell you what it said?" he asked. She could sense that he didn't believe her. He suspected that she had just thrown the letter away unopened and was now denying it. Sibling rivalry was still alive and well. Jayden nodded politely and gave a wooden smile.

"In...prison..." Nick eyed his sister nervously like a rabbit ready to run if she reacted to any of the words he intended to use. "Well...I did a degree in chemistry and then a masters in...actually, none of that matters. I had time on my hands so..." Even he could see that it wasn't the right track to go down. Any extended time on his hands was his own fault. Nick laboured on, "I've been working for a Christian organisation since I got out last year, lecturing and speaking about the harmful effects of drugs. I work mainly with teenagers, addicts and those at risk of becoming addicted. I leave for America in two days. I've got a two-year contract to do the same sort of thing with teens in the cities over there. I give a testimony of my own...experiences and then hit them with the facts of what all that stuff does to your head."

He stopped, looking at his sister for a reaction, anything that would act as a gauge for what was currently going through her mind. "Ed said that I scared you. I sincerely apologise for that. I wanted to see you and wasn't sure how to go about it. The letter..."

"I didn't see the letter!" Jayden raised her voice and heard the faint shuffle of Ed outside the door. He had left it slightly ajar, knowing that the heavy oak would not necessarily allow her cries for help to escape. The inappropriate thought crossed his mind that someone could be murdered in there unnoticed, squashed quickly by the sobering thought of McLean's death only a matter of metres up the steps from that same room. Ed sat on the cold stone outside the door; his legs stretched out and his back and head resting on the wall behind where Jayden sat. It was ridiculous to think that she could draw strength from his proximity, but he hoped anyway and went back to praying for her, his dark head bowed and his fringe falling forward in his eyes in uncharacteristic disarray.

Nick raised his head in placation. "Ok, ok, you didn't see the letter. I'm sorry."

"What do you want from me?" Jayden asked, standing up. "Why are you here? How did you find me?"

Nick wisely stayed seated. "I see Mum every couple of months..."

"Liar!" Jayden cried. "Aunty would never let you near her!"

Nick looked down at his hands knotting and unknotting a piece of thread that he had pulled from his green puffer jacket.

"I visit when she's in respite care. She gave me your address last time I saw her."

Jayden shook her head angrily now. "She can't even remember her own name. I don't believe you!"

Nick looked away once and then stood up. "I am truly sorry, Lily. I am so sorry for everything. I wanted...I don't know what I wanted. I shouldn't have come." *Disappointment* and *Misery* crowded round him compounding his agony. "I was wrong, I was so wrong. Nothing I say will *ever* make it right. I guess I wanted you to see that I had changed, that salvation comes even to people like me. I did a prison Alpha course and gave my life to Christ. He's helped me turn it around and put it all to good use, all the wicked stuff, Lil. It has a purpose. I'm not asking for your forgiveness. Heck, it's taken me nine years to forgive myself, so I don't expect you to. I wanted you to know that *I'm sorry* and that I mean it." Nick moved slowly towards the door, understanding that the meeting was over. At the last minute, he turned and said quietly to his broken sister, "You lost everything because of me. I *do* know that."

Then he was gone, striding down the long stone corridor and out into the surprise twinkling of sunshine. There were tears in his eyes, but his heart felt strangely lighter. He knew that he would probably never see his sister again and that it had always lurked as a frightening possibility. Some part of him had hoped that they could forge something from the ashes, but it had always been a long shot. His mother had been very lucid the last time he visited. She had understood that he was leaving and that if the two-year contract went well, he might never return to the land of his birth. But towards the end of the visit as she was growing tired, she had patted his hand and called him 'Dan' and it had broken his heart.

Ed stood quickly and went into the vestry. It was wood panelled and dark; a large leaded window obscured by a flying buttress holding up the side of the building. The stone floor had been covered with an ancient maroon rug with gold inlay, worn by the rubber soled feet of generations of clergymen. Jayden had poked the toes of her boots underneath one edge and stared down at her hidden feet aimlessly. Ed had heard Nick's last words, acknowledging that he had caused this woman to lose absolutely everything and from their conversations over the past few days, had known that the man felt deeply for what his selfish youth had caused.

Jayden looked up at Ed finally and he was stunned

by the clearness in her face. She looked almost childlike and beatific as he stared down at her, a slight crease in his brow. Unshed tears glinted in her eyes, but she seemed completely in control despite her ordeal. Then to his surprise, she smiled. "I didn't lose everything," she said, "not really. Just five big things. But not everything."

CHAPTER TWENTY-FIVE

"Why have you got that colour shirt on?" Jayden asked Ed as he sat with her in her living room. He had walked her home, poured them both a large glass of red wine and then sat with his arm possessively around her shoulders. Nick's letter had somehow been pushed underneath the front door mat at some point in the previous week and was crumpled and slightly damp. It sat unopened on the dining table with the electricity bill which had accompanied it.

Jayden closed her eyes, enjoying the feel of Ed's cloth shirt under her right palm, the steady thrum of his heartbeat and knowing that it all had to end. Ed rubbed at the centre of the purple shirt, feeling nervous sweat pooling at the base of his back. "I need to take up my new office soon. The new vicar starts at St Jude's tomorrow. You'll really like him. He's quite young and enthusiastic. He'll shake things up." Ed tried to smile at Jayden as she sat up, looking ashen and shocked.

"Please don't go?" she whispered and Ed's brow creased in fear. He sat forward and turned in his seat so that he could look at Jayden full in the face and read her expression, not that he thought it would help much. Where this woman was concerned, he felt utterly clueless.

Jayden suddenly dipped forward and Ed grabbed at her shoulders in concern as she seemed to bend in half over her knees. She moaned and he slipped off the seat and knelt in front of her wondering what was wrong. "Your wife," Jayden said sadly. "I'm sorry. This has all been so surreal this past few weeks that I keep kidding myself that we have a future. It's ok, I understand."

Ed seized Jayden by both shoulders and made her sit up and look at him. His handsome features were screwed up in a look of disbelief. "I don't have a wife, Jayd. I have no idea why you keep referring to one either."

"Raff said..."

"Raff!" Ed spat his brother's name with an angry edge to his voice. "You really need to stop listening to that guy. He talks utter crap, Jayd!"

"So, are you divorced?" Jayden looked so innocent that it exasperated Ed to the point where he could have screamed.

"No, I've never been married. It's the Church. It's my *calling*, my faith. He calls it my 'wife.' He's always done it and he knows I hate it but it's easier just to ignore him."

"The Church? The Church is your wife?" Jayden was feeling emotionally drained and unbelievably dim.

Ed pulled her face up to look at him, trying to get her attention again, aware that he was quickly losing her to a veil of tired confusion.

"I partnered with them," Jayden said, sounding utterly exhausted.

Ed pulled a face and looked at her quizzically. "What? Who?"

"The demons," she replied sadly, "the negative stuff and the lies about myself. *Grief* and *Shame* and *Disgust*, sometimes *Death* and *Guilt*. *Guilt* was always there hovering. It's my fault. I partnered with them in my own destruction."

She sounded as though she was rambling and Ed became concerned for her mental state. He ran his fingers up the side of her face, compassion pouring from his eyes into her soul and warming her through like summer sunshine.

"When you experience hurt like mine, you accidentally let them in. Jesus says to forgive, but I didn't want to hear that, I haven't been ready. But they crowded round me, *Anger, Self-pity, Resentment, Intimidation*, they comforted me and told me what I wanted to hear. I partnered with them. Don't you get it? I willingly partnered with them."

Ed did get it. He nodded, genuinely acknowledging her pain and understanding her dilemma. "I get it," he said simply, smoothing her hair back from her sweating brow. "It's ok. You can ask them to leave. Jesus gives you the right to tell them to go. Let me help you?"

Jayden leaned her head against Ed while he prayed for her, rebuked the swirling hoards in the apex of the roof and heard their strangled final breaths through his spiritual ears as the abyss sucked them back in, ending their nine-year reign of terror. "They've gone," Jayden said finally, sitting up and wiping her nose on the sleeve of her blouse. "It's so quiet."

Ed went out to get fish and chips from the lower end of the High Street while Jayden had a shower and sorted herself out. She struggled to keep her cast dry, but the lure of the cleansing water was cathartic. The spray pounded her head and back, washing away the misery and agony along with the filthy residue of the familial spirits who had claimed the rights to Jayden's existence, sneaking in and taking up residence with a hastily and falsely given permission. Jayden sat at the table by the window, watching Ed while he sourced plates and cutlery. She ate with gusto like a starving woman released from prison and presented with a banquet table.

Ed smiled fondly at her, but after a while became nervous, plucking at his shirt front with shaking fingers, as he set his cutlery down gently on the table. "Jayd, I need to talk to you about some things."

Jayden's heart bounded in fear, righting itself when the new lease of life which coursed through her veins censured it and gave her confidence. Ed looked increasingly afraid and Jayden waited for the awful truth which would end their friendship-relationship-whatever it was. The handsome cleric sat back in his chair, agony and fear radiating off him. "Jayd, when the Reverend McLean phoned the acting bishop to ask for help, he actually got the new bishop, who was down in Lincoln visiting and answered the office phone, quite by chance. The new bishop decided that he would send someone he trusted to take a look at what was going on. The retiring incumbent had hinted at certain things not being quite right, so he thought he might get it checked out. I went to stay with Raff, but the curate sent to investigate, rang to tell me that there was a death in his family. He couldn't go. I had no choice. The vicar of St Jude's had never met me and so I stood in as his curate. Jayden, there were huge things wrong."

Ed ran a shaking hand across his face. "I found financial discrepancies and other problems, ingrained and part of the fabric of the church. It was a real travesty. Nothing was being done right. Brian was obviously out of control and struggling and McLean had done nothing to help. If anything, he had compounded the man's problems. It was a mess. I had to do something..."

"So you killed him?" Jayden looked completely confused and her assumption might have been hilarious if it hadn't been so inappropriate. Ed gritted his teeth and pressed on, willing her to understand so that he only had to say this once and then wait for her reaction.

"No. Back up. Brian killed him. Remember?"

Emboldened by her nod, he continued, "The night he died, I challenged him about a donation - a bequest - that had gone missing around the time he bought his holiday home in Skegness. The accountant who used to audit everything was a friend of his and was recently prosecuted for fraud. McLean became furious with me and told me it was none of my business. I had no alternative and so I had to..."

"*Not* kill him," Jayden said and shook her head. She sounded so childlike and innocent that Ed smiled at her and leaning across, ran his left hand up the back of her neck and into her long hair, instantly tangling his fingers in the myriad glossy curls.

"No," he said gently, "*not* kill him. Jayd, I had to tell him that it *was* my business... because I *am* the bishop."

Jayden looked at him with her brow furrowed. She felt empty inside although more peaceful than she had for nine long years. It wasn't so much that she was numb, but more that she could no longer hear the whispered criticisms and jibes from the emotional demons who had familiarly haunted her soul. Her head felt blissfully clear. She wanted to lie down finally and sleep, feeling sure that it would be dreamless and fulfilling. She looked hard at Ed's purple shirt and tried to take it all in. He was the bishop, the big boss, the one whom Reverend McLean had openly spent hours swooning over and conspiring to meet. He had been under the old man's nose the whole time, hosing out dustbins and clearing leaves from the gutters.

It was incongruous and ridiculous. To Ed's surprise, Jayden began to chuckle as Lily McGowan's spirit leaked out and found the situation entertaining. Jayden laughed and laughed and laughed until she was exhausted. As Ed finally allowed his nerves to relax, he delighted in the beauty of the woman in front of him. Lily McGowan was truly stunning as she flexed her personality, unfettered for the first time in almost a decade. The mask that was Jayden Mitchell slipped irrevocably away, surplus to requirement in the life that was ahead of this woman, who no longer had demons on her shoulder or anywhere else in her life.

Up in Lincoln Cathedral, the famed imp continued to sit on his stone perch surveying the visiting tourists below. His tiny teeth gleamed grey and pointy in his shadowy maw. Myriad demons circled his throne paying tribute to his wicked self, before settling back down on the shoulders of their hosts, carried forth into the world to make mischief and cause mayhem. The imp was ages old, sitting out his punishment in spectacular silence and isolation, hidden to most but visible to a few. He had sat for centuries but was, in fact, even older than that. He was as old as the First Adam, who had partnered with his own demons, *Grief, Disappointment* and *Guilt*, wearing them on his shoulders like a shroud as they drove him into despair for his disobedience.

The imp heard the distant sound of Lily McGowan's tinkling laughter and felt her blessed relief with a flash of anger that rippled his stone body. A crash clanged into the cavernous space as something fell over, masking the otherworldly roar of temper that echoed in the underworld.

As the bowed and willing cathedral guide led yet another group of tourists to the bottom of his throne and pointed upwards, she stopped momentarily with her hand partly raised in the air and a number of pairs of eyes faced her way in surprise. "Goodness me," she remarked incredulously, "it sounds ridiculous but I think our Lincoln Imp looks even crosser today."

The visitors laughed between themselves and humoured the elderly, fluffy haired guide as the imp glowered and glowered.

Dear Reader,

I would be really grateful if you would take the time to leave a review at the site where you purchased this novel and at Goodreads.com

It doesn't have to be an essay, just a few short sentences about what you liked or enjoyed would be appreciated. Reviews help other readers decide to purchase my novels and you will be allowing me to reach a wider audience in an otherwise difficult publishing environment.

Thank you in anticipation.

K T Bowes

ABOUT THE AUTHOR

K T Bowes lives in New Zealand between the Hakarimata Ranges and the Waikato River, not far from Hana's house. She is married with four children who are off around the world doing wonderful things of their own. A stroppy ginger cat lives with her and there is usually a crazy horse or two living in her paddock behind her house.

You can follow her blogs on Twitter @hanadurose
www.facebook.com/hanadurose and
http://ktbowes.blogspot.com/

Printed in Great Britain
by Amazon